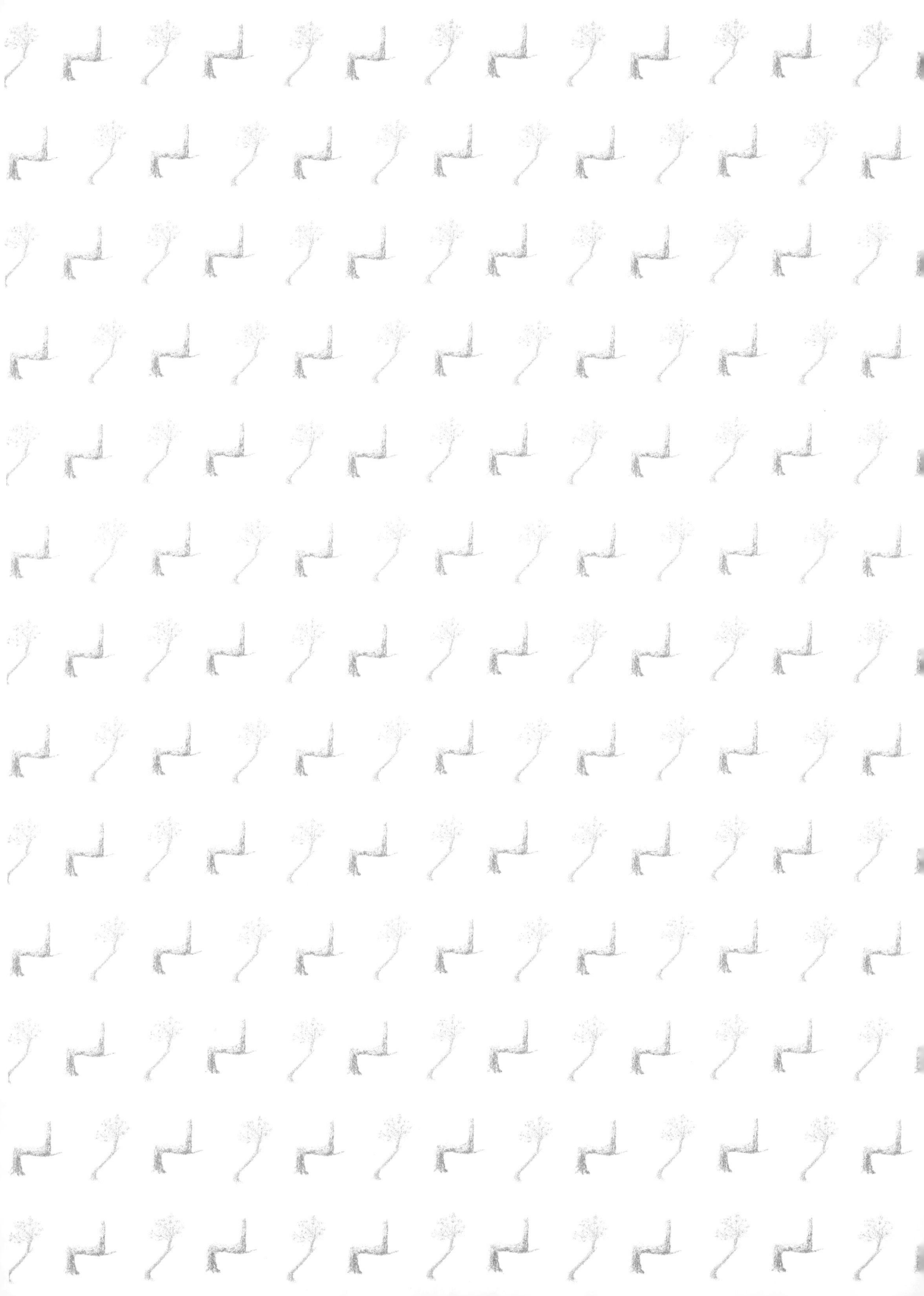

Ute Indian Prayer Trees

Of the Pikes Peak Region

Ute Indian Prayer Trees

Trees

Of the Pikes Peak Region

John Wesley Anderson

Honoring the Past

CIRCLE STAR
PUBLISHING

Shaping the Future

CIRCLE STAR PUBLISHING
COLORADO SPRINGS, COLORADO

Ute Indian Prayer Trees of the Pikes Peak Region

Anderson, John Wesley

Revised Edition

February 1, 2021

ISBN: 978-1-943829-26-2

Library of Congress Control Number: 2021900303

Previously published by Old Colorado City Historical Society

✹

Publisher's Cataloging-in-Publication data

Names: Anderson, John Wesley, author.

Title: Ute Indian prayer trees of the Pikes Peak region / John Wesley Anderson.

Description: Includes bibliographical references. | Colorado Springs, CO: Circle Star Publishing,

an imprint of Rhyolite Press LLC, 2021.

Identifiers: ISBN: 9781943829262 (Hardcover)

Subjects: LCSH Indians of North America--Spiritual life--Colorado. | Ute Indians--Colorado--Antiquities. | Trees--Colorado. | Historic trees--Colorado. | Trees--Symbolic aspects. | Ethnoecology. | BISAC HISTORY / Native American | NATURE / Regional | HISTORY / United States / State & Local / West (AK, CA, CO, HI, ID, MT, NV, UT, WY)

Classification: LCC E99.U8 A53 2021 | DDC 979.004/974576--dc23

✹

Book layout & design: Susie Schorsch   Cover design: Donald Kallaus

Published in the United States of America

Circle Star Publishing
P.O. Box 60144
Colorado Springs, Colorado 80960

Dedication

To the Seventh Generation; this is your time, this is your place and these sacred trees are a gift from your tribal elders.

Wisdom of the Elders

"We must protect the forest for our children, grandchildren and the children yet to be born. We must protect the forest for those who can't speak for themselves such as the birds, animal, fish and trees."
Qwatsinas – Nazalk Nation

Nine Leadership Secrets from the Ute Tribal Elders:

1. *There is but one Creator of all that is or ever was or ever will be*

2. *Tava (Pikes Peak) is sacred; the Creator has the sun rise there first*

3. *Morning's first light is a gift from the Creator; use each of His gifts wisely*

4. *Respect the Elders for they know the way; Elders and children always eat first*

5. *There is no rich, no poor, I can only be rich if I am known to possess many friends*

6. *Sunwise is Right Thinking; know where it is you stand, life is a circle, share the chant*

7. *Never underestimate the power of storytelling; it teaches how one should strive to live*

8. *There is no greater honor for a warrior than to die bravely in battle fending one's tribe*

9. *Seek the Póogats, experts who have been there before; for they know the say it is you wish to go*

Photograph page x: **La Foret Trailmarker Tree** *is located along the left bank of Kettle Creek in the Black Forest. It points northeast towards the Cherokee Trail. The tree is located below the Blue Spruce Cabin north of the stone labyrinth on property today owned by the La Foret Conference & Event Center, El Paso County, Colorado. The tree was found within a few feet of where a moose was photographed standing sentry at the beginning of the opening ceremony for the first Ute Indian Prayer Tree Retreat in 2013.*

Table of Contents

Acknowledgments

This book was truly a team effort, made possible only through the unwavering support of my family, my wife Brenda and daughter Laynie, a host of personal friends, and the trusted partnership of the Old Colorado City Historical Society (OCCHS); notably Past President Sharon Swint, Archivist Tom Daniels and Treasurer Susie Schorsch, to whom I owe a special debt of gratitude. Susie has championed this book project from its inception, sponsored luncheons for the Ute people attending our annual Ute Prayer Tree gathering, helped with editing and preparation for publishing.

The Ute believe you can only be rich if you are known to possess many friends. From those words of wisdom, I am a very fortunate man to count among my friends two personal friends who have taken almost every step along the journey with me, Phil Tinsley and Vern Kuykendall. Phil and Vern have shared this adventure with me, from our first hikes through the Black Forest, our first trip to the Southern Ute Reservation, working to do whatever needed to be done to help host the Ute at La Foret, all while contributing their abundant intellect, energy and contagious sense of humor along the way. I also want to thank Rhonda Thompson who provided our first edits to the draft manuscript to make sure this book was worthy of the subject.

Lastly, I want to thank two Ute spiritual leaders from the Southern Ute Reservation. Nathan Strong Elk, former Executive Director of the Southern Ute Cultural Center and Museum, for sharing his spiritual insights and leadership in support of our first annual Ute Indian Prayer Tree Retreat at La Foret in 2013. Lastly, I wish to extend my most heartfelt appreciation to Dr. James M. Jefferson, Ute Tribal Elder, for sharing his spiritual wisdom, guidance and trust in me to tell this story about these sacred trees left behind by his Ute Tribal ancestors so very long ago. I will remember Dr. Jefferson's unwavering support of "our mission," so aptly captured the words of his wise counsel, *"Now is the time to take risks; otherwise it will all be forgotten."*

My friends at the Old Colorado City Historical Society (OCCHS) told me early on in this project, that writing a book is a team effort. Looking back, I wholeheartedly concur and must express my deepest appreciation to my following teammates:

Brenda Vaughn Anderson	Old Colorado City Historical Society
Laynie Reid Anderson	Pikes Peak Library District
Patti Beady	Jim, Debi, Kris & Jeni Reed
Colorado Springs Pioneers Museum	Suzanne Schorsch
Les, Betty & Rose Davis	Bill & Linda Scott
Thomas Daniels	Dave & Ruth Spencer
Bob DeWitt & Dorothy Merlo	Terry Stokka
Dr. James M. Jefferson	Rhonda Thompson
Vern Kuykendall	Phil Tinsley
El Paso County Parks Department	Ralph & Calise Townsend
Paula & Rollie Johnson	Southern Ute Cultural Center & Museum
La Foret Conference & Event Center	Gary Zeigler & Amy Finger
Mango Moose of Gleneagle	

Thank you, this truly was our journey, Towaoc (Ute word for thank you).
John Wesley Anderson, Sheriff (ret.) El Paso County, Colorado (1995-2003)

Introduction

At the heart of the Shining Mountains stands a mountain the ancient Ute knew as Tava. It was the most sacred of all places to the Ute because the sun, which gives forth life from the Creator, always rose there first. The Ute believed that at the beginning of time, the Creator made the Shining Mountains; then, He created the animals, and when He was finished He created The Nuche, The People. The Ute believed the Shining Mountains were created by the Creator to sustain, not just them, but all The People. To the Ute people, life began in the Shining Mountains.

There are different variations of the Ute creation story. One entitled *Senawahv's People*, published by the Ute Indian Museum located in Montrose, Colorado, teaches the Ute:

> *In the days before ancient times, there were no people in any part of the world. One day Senawahv, the Creator, began to cut sticks and place them in a large bag. He gave the bag to Coyote (Senawahv's younger brother) and said, 'Carry these over the far hills to the valleys beyond. You must not open the bag until you reach the sacred grounds.'*
>
> *Coyote was young and foolish, consumed with curiosity. As soon as he was over the first hill and out of sight, he decided to peek into the bag. 'That could hurt nothing,' he thought. When Coyote untied the bag many people came out, all of them speaking different languages. He tried to catch them and get them into the bag, but they scattered in every direction.*
>
> *By the time Coyote closed the bag, it was almost empty. He hurried on to the sacred valley and opened the bag, releasing the few people who remained. These were the Ute.*
>
> *When Senawahv learned what had happened, he was very angry with Coyote. 'Those you let escape will forever be at war with the Ute,' he said. 'They will forever try to gain the land from their neighbors. But the Ute, though few in number, will be the mightiest and most valiant of heart. They will be able to defeat the rest.'*

The Shining Mountains are the snow capped Rocky Mountain Range from Northern New Mexico through Colorado north to Wyoming and west to Utah. The Ute welcomed newcomers to the Shining Mountains including other Native Tribes, early explorers, adventurers, French fur trappers, gold prospectors, and later the pioneer settlers who began to arrive in their covered wagons by the droves. The Spanish name for Tava was Sierra Almagre. Lt. Zebulon Pike wrote Grand Peak upon his map in 1806 to chart the location of this majestic 14,115 foot mountain peak that would one day bear honor to his name, Pikes Peak. Since the beginning of time, Almagre, Grand Peak or Pikes Peak was known first by the Ute as Sun Mountain, Tava.

Ute men thought it shameful to allow the morning's first light to shine through the tepee opening and catch them wrapped in their warm blankets. Although the Ute were generally known to be a peaceful people, especially toward the early pioneers of the 1860s, they were highly skilled and fearlessly trained warriors who understood the advantage gained fighting from a defensive position. The Ute were darker in skin color and shorter in height than most other Native Americans, the tallest warriors measuring only about 5'6" in height. They were a very strong and sturdy people. Ute warriors were extremely skilled when mounted on horseback and had studied the art of war craft starting as young boys just learning to walk.

The Ute who cultivated many Prayer Trees found today in the Pikes Peak Region were an intelligent, resourceful and industrious people. Moreover, they were a deeply spiritual people who believed they were one with nature, a gift from the Creator, their Father. The Ute believed all life came from Mother Earth and were committed to living in harmony with everything made by the Creator. At the end of life they would ascend before their Creator, with whom they hoped to spend eternity in the afterlife with all His creations. Accompanying their deep respect for nature, the Ute held an immense understanding of science, including astrology, geography, horticulture, hunting, animal husbandry and medicine. The story of the Ute Indian Prayer Trees cannot just be about sacred trees, it must also examine the Ute, their culture and their sacred places.

The Ute culture is rich with artifacts demonstrating their passion for music, often played on instruments they crafted by hand. Their beautiful art is demonstrated by an unparalleled skill woven into their extraordinary basketry. The Ute basket-making skills remain unrivaled to this day, in much the same way that the Navajo blankets have no equal. Ute baskets, made from all-natural fibers, were not only beautiful, but were so tightly woven they could effectively hold water. Their unique designs, colors, weaves and spiral shapes, all contributed to helping Ute grandmothers teach their daughters and grandchildren about their beloved Ute ancestors and told of their rich heritage.

Among some of the most accomplished Native American hunters and marksmen anywhere in North America were the Ute men and the buckskins tanned by the Ute women were one of the finest quality ever known. Hides tanned by Ute women were highly coveted not just by other the Native American tribes, but by the early French trappers who made their livelihood trading in the world's finest quality fur pelts and animal hides. The early Spanish explorers also highly valued the Ute animal hides in trade.

According to Southern Ute Tribal Elder, Dr. James Jefferson, most of the Ute tribal members developed some special skill that would prove beneficial for their tribe. As young members of the tribe, they learned how to become subject matter experts in hunting, defense, medicine, caring for horses, tanning leather, moving a camp efficiently from one place to another or modifying a tree, all to benefit the tribe. This practice of acquiring the prerequisite knowledge, skill and ability to become highly proficient in one or more domains would contribute to the overall health, welfare and sustainment of the Ute people, and it remained an important part of the Ute culture for hundreds of years.

The Ute, like most Native American cultures, had no alphabet, so they had no written language. Their interdependence on their Elders to pass along their oral history and serve as their tribal subject matter experts worked well for them as long as they had access to the Elders, and there was a need for that knowledge, skill or ability. This is why, according to Dr. Jefferson, the cultural tree modification practices of the Ute people have sadly been lost to history. When the Ute were forced onto the reservation, they may have felt they as a people no longer had a need to learn Culturally Modified Tree (CMT) practices that had been acquired and handed down over countless generations. This advanced knowledge, these unique skills, this vanishing ability was no longer required.

The other tragic reality for nearly all Native Americans was that once they made contact with the Europeans, contagious deadly diseases, such as smallpox, spread with alarming speed and devastating results. The Ute, as with other indigenous peoples of the Americas, lost many tribal members, including entire families, to these rapidly spreading diseases for which they had no immunity or medicine to cure. The greatest losses among the Ute were tragically suffered by the children and their Tribal Elders. They were the teachers of their culture and the students who were expected to carry their culture forward.

While talking with Ute Tribal Elder, Dr. Jefferson, and sharing the many photos of Ute Indian Prayer Trees we had taken on walks together through the Shining Mountains, he sadly acknowledged the Ute had lost much of their knowledge of how these trees were cultivated. He did pass on many of his memories, including how these trees typically belonged to one family, and although each of the Ute families might all use common practices, such as peeling the bark, extracting the pine pitch or staking down the tree in a certain direction, each Ute family's Prayer Tree could turn out to be much different from another family's tree. Dr. Jefferson explained that there would have been what he referred to as "artistic differences."

The material for this book is intended to serve the reader as an introductory guide, not as a reference text book. It is a collection of photographs and information I gathered while making a journey of discovery of Ute Prayer Trees. It begins with a background on how I became interested in the subject. Then it lays a general foundation for Culturally Modified Trees (CMT) and Ute Prayer Trees (UPT). Next it covers a historic overview of the Ute people and their early contact with Europeans in the Pikes Peak Region. It offers readers an opportunity to discover UPTs on their own in the Pikes Peak Region and to gain a clearer understanding of "Why this matters," as Dr. Jefferson often explains.

My research on UPT remains very much a work in progress. Much credit extends to the people who helped in this journey, while any mistakes remain those of my own as the author. As explained by Dr. Jefferson, just because someone thinks differently from another, does not necessarily make what either of them say wrong, adding that their belief or thinking was right to that person. As the author, I fully recognize many educational "gaps" exist especially with respect to the two critical areas of "how" and "why" these spiritual and navigational trees were cultivated. Placing types of trees in categories will vary between individuals, but what remains constant is the importance of these trees. This book represents my best attempt to understand these trees, hoping others will continue to build upon this work and advance the appreciation of these sacred trees and the people who cultivated these trees in the shadow of the Peak. In retrospect, I don't know if I found these trees or they found me. What I do know is my life has been immeasurably enriched through countless friendships that have been built, and existing friendships that have been extended during this, my fascinating journey back in time, attempting to absorb a tiny sliver of the rich history and culture of the Ute Nation. Similar to many other indigenous people around the world, the Ute cultivated trees for various purposes including navigational, medicinal, nutritional, burial, and many utilitarian benefits. Modifications to these sacred trees, by the Ute, were done with a sincere reverence to Mother Earth, and their cultivation practices always began with a sacred prayer to their Creator.

Right: **Snowcapped Tava (Pikes Peak).** *This photo was taken from the west ridge line of Ute Valley Park in Colorado Springs. The foot trail leading west up to and crosses between these two white rock formations is well-worn, with evidence of more recent usage, as well as previous Native American usage. From the top of this ridge one has a commanding 360° view which would have provided an excellent platform for observation and signaling. The Spanish Explorers and French Fur Trappers found that small hand mirrors were one of the more popular trade items for the Ute, especially the men as they were highly desirable for sending signals from one distant location to another. Ute scouts also used smoke from campfires during the day or campfires at night, as an effective form of communication and their signals were known to be so detailed they could communicate rapidly across a series of highpoints when friendly or enemy riders were approaching, provide the name of the trail or pass they were traveling or even provide the number of enemy warriors that were approaching.*

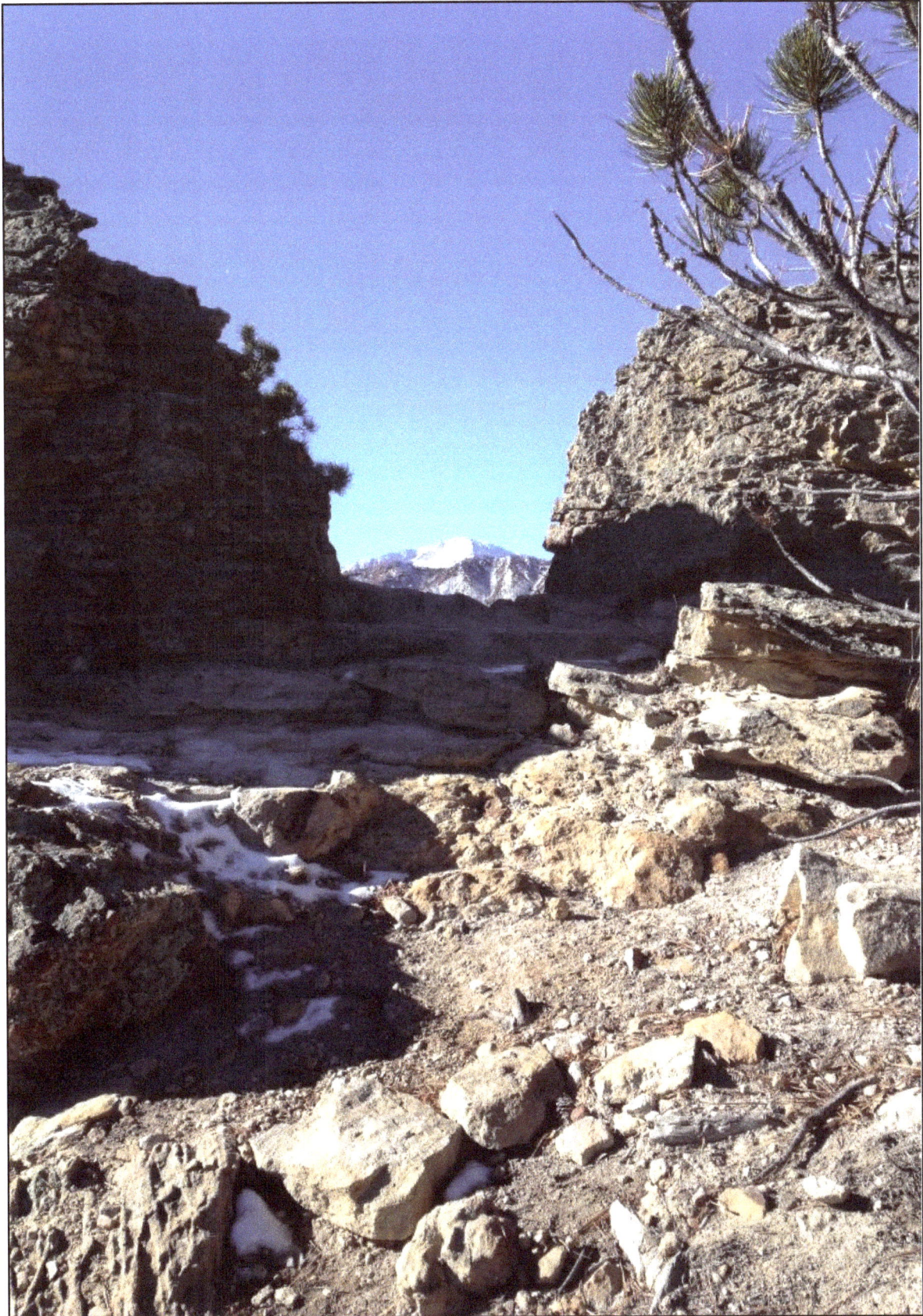

Right: **Aspen Tepees**. This photo is of two modern tepees that were erected using the traditional design of Ute. Ute men always slept with their head towards the north and the tepees opening to the east to catch the morning's first light, a gift from the Creator. Ute tepees traditionally include 6-8 family members and were clustered in grouping of 8-10 unless they were gathering for ceremonial or hunting purposes. They were traditionally laid out in the configuration of the Pleiades Star Cluster, known as the Seven Sisters. Each of the seven primary stars was represented on the ground with a designated location for the tribal leadership, including the Chief or sub-chief, Tribal Elders and the Medicine Man. This organization was purposeful as well as helpful, particularly if one needed to report approaching danger or to find someone. The sacred medicine wheel, which provided spiritual and navigational guidance, was located first then the other six predetermined locations were laid out for the tepees. The Ute burned small fires inside their tepees in the winter, the smoke from the pine trees often blacken the tops of the tepees, which from a distance helped identify a camp as being Ute. This photo, taken in fall, a time when the Ute men would be hunting game and women would be preserving food. The white bark of the Aspen trees offered an ideal medium to carve a short term message as the split in the white bark turns black rapidly allowing for any man-made imperfections to stand out from the other Aspen trees. Messages left on Aspen trees were more short-lived due to the life span of the Aspen. All across the 40 acre property of this mountain retreat the owners of Dancing Coyote Canyon have taken great care to live as the Ute did in harmony with nature leaving the least impact on the land as possible. This property is located near Lake George and is abundantly rich with wild game (deer, bear and elk) and is rich in Ute Indian Prayer Trees surrounded by multiple ancient Native American archaeological sites including rock water basins. This photo was taken in the Aspen Grove of Dancing Coyote Canyon, north of the Eleven Mile State Recreational Campground, in Park County, Colorado.

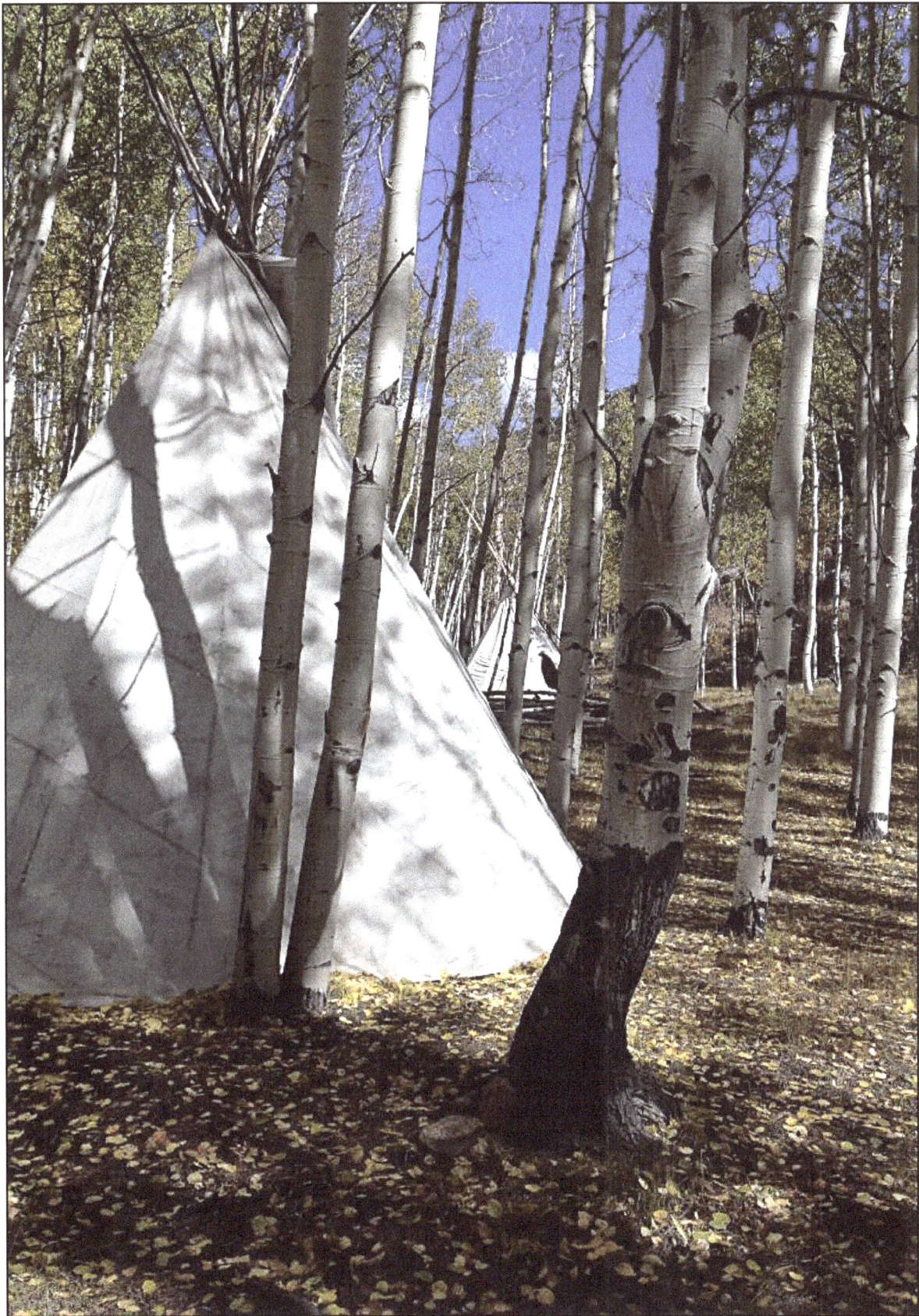

Top Right Photograph: This stone projectile point was discovered in the 1960's by the author on his family's ranch in eastern El Paso County, Colorado. This arrowhead design is what is known as a Lancelot Arrowhead and may be attributed to either the Cheyenne or Arapahoe Indians as it was discovered within sixteen miles of what was their Reservation when Colorado first became a Territory in 1861.

Center Photograph: This beautiful clear quartz crystal arrowhead was inadvertently unearthed on the Arrow C Ranch by the ranch owner Elaine Cain while a horse barn was being constructed. The ranch is located in Douglas County on the northern most edge of Black Forest with a spectacular view of Tava (Pikes Peak). Clear crystal arrowheads are incredibly rare and the only similar arrowheads that could be found during the research for this book are on display at the Indian museum at Cheaha State Park in Alabama, a mountainous region that was at one time a large Creek Indian area. This arrowhead measures nearly two inches in length and the craftsmanship is absolutely flawless. From the thin, fluted design, with bifacial percussion flaking, this projectile point may be classified as a Clovis point, which if correct could date the projectile point to the Paleoindian period which was around 13,500 years ago. A major Clovis cache consisting of 83 Clovis stone tools that were scientifically determined to be 13,000 to 13,500 years old were discovered northwest of this site in 2009 in Boulder, Colorado. There is a possibility this crystal arrowhead is a ceremonial arrowhead and the stone may have originated on or near Crystal Peak since it is one of the largest source of clear quartz crystal in what is today Colorado. The Cheyenne, who would have hunted bison in this area up until the mid-19th Century, were known for a sacred ceremony which recognized sacred arrows. The famous Cheyenne War Chief White Thunder, whose daughter Owl Woman married William Bent, is believed to have been later given the name "Keeper of the Sacred Arrows."

Lower Photograph: This hatchet head stone tool was discovered partially buried in the sandy top soil on the author's family ranch. The tool is the head of a hatchet or hand ax and when found the wooden handle had been worn or weathered completely away; however, the white masonry material which was used to affix the hatchet or ax head to the handle remained intact. This hatched head is most likely attributed to the Cheyenne or Arapahoe as it was found within twenty miles west of their former Indian Reservation. It is believed that this type of stone hatchet may have been what was used to strike the bark of the Ponderosa Pine Tree to begin the process of peeling the bark for ceremonial, medicinal or nutritional purposes until metal axes were introduced into the Pikes Peak Region by the early miners and settlers.

Rock Basins: This rock water basin was one of many found clustered together with dozens of Ute Indian Prayer Trees discovered on private property northwest of Eleven Mile Reservoir, in Park County, Colorado. Several of these water basins were connected by narrow troughs etched into the granite rock intended to catch and retain rainwater or snow melt. This area was a known sacred Ute hunting area for elk, deer, antelope and bison. The Ute were expert tanners of animal hides, especially their soft buckskin which was highly coveted by other Native Americans, as well as the early Spanish Explores and French Trappers. The hides were soaked in a mixture of ash from the campfires and water then the hair was scraped from the hides with rough stones. Large stone tools, such as the mano and metate used to grind food by hand, were too heavy to carry from camp to camp and were often left in place for later use (a mano was found by the author's stepfather when he was a boy near this Eleven Mile Canyon and is in the author's collection). This land is managed by Dancing Coyote Canyon which strives to combine a unique mixture of practitioners that offer creative healing and wisdom retreats designed to help a person relax and recharge. These rock artifacts were left in place where they were found.

Trailmarker Gore Pass: This Ute Prayer Tree is a classic Ute Trailmarker Tree and points north towards a trail that traces Gore Creek up and through Gore Pass (summit elevation 9,524 feet). This Ute Trailmarker Tree displays the classical one 30° bend, a withered primary trunk or spur and the distinct peeled bark pattern where the bark is cut at the top and torn away from the trunk at the bottom, consistent with dozens of Ute Trailmarker Trees discovered in many other counties throughout Colorado. Gore Creek is a tributary of the White River, which runs through what was the White River Ute Indian Reservation, near today's Meeker, Colorado. This tree was discovered on private property in East Vail, Eagle County, Colorado. The photo shows I-70 west of Vail Pass in the background.

Chapter 1 - The Journey Begins
There is but one Creator of all that is or ever was or ever will be.

Looking back, the beginnings of my interest in Ute Prayer trees was a journey that started many years ago. As a child I was interested in anything that was unusual in nature. My early adventures of hunting rocks that had been made into arrowheads would awaken my interest in trees that had been altered by man. My lessons growing up on a ranch and being taught the difference between a good snake and a dangerous snake would help later in my understanding of good and bad in people and how to not judge the total by the actions of one. I would also learn that what one person believes is true can be different to another in different cultures. The respect I had for the older members of my family and what they taught me would only deepen as I learned the wisdom of the Ute Elders.

Hunting arrowheads on the small ranch where I grew up in Colorado, about forty-five miles east of Pikes Peak, was always an adventure. On most days, standing on our ranch land, you could see the Spanish Peaks, miles off to the Southwest. But on a really clear day, the Sangre de Cristo Mountain Range could come into view, standing majestically on further to the west just north of the New Mexico border. Sangre de Cristo, Spanish for the Blood of Christ, always makes me think of those rugged Spanish Conquistadors who named this mountain and the San Juan Mountain Range. When the Spanish explorers crossed these snowcapped peaks four hundred years ago, they were on a quest for the lost cities of gold, for Cibola, in search of El Dorado.

During the winter months, when morning's first light would strike the tops of the rugged snowcapped Pikes Peak or the Sangre de Cristo or the two Spanish Peaks, it looked like someone had flipped on a light switch. The Spanish knew these two mountains as Dos Hermanos or The Two Brothers and the Native Americans called them Wahatoya meaning Breasts of the World, but today our limited imagination forces us to refer to them simply as the East or West Spanish Peak. As a kid, if you stared at these snowcapped peaks long enough, the reflection off the mountains would glisten so brightly they could water your eyes. It is easy to see why the Ute Indians referred to these rugged snowcapped mountains as the Shining Mountains.

We purchased our ranch land in the 1960's and it was one of the original 160 acre tracts that had been initially acquired almost a hundred years earlier through the 1862 Homestead Act which had been enacted toward the beginning of the American Civil War to encourage western expansion and fill the land from sea to sea. The fact there were already hundreds of thousands of Native Americans, the citizens of the First Nation, already here well-established in the perceived emptiness of the West was of little, to no concern, to those moving westward during the mid-nineteenth Century.

You could never get lost hiking across on our ranch land. 160 acres isn't that big, only one quarter square mile, but Pikes Peak was always on our western horizon. Whenever you would glance up, that majestic mountain was always there. The mountain had inspired Katherine Lee Bates to write the words to her poem *America the Beautiful* after returning from a trip to the summit during the summer of 1893. To me and so many others before and after me, Pikes Peak stood out as a shining beacon, an anchor to let you know where you were, to help guide you to where you wanted to go.

Two distinct memories stand out from my childhood. One involved my grandfather, Charles Davis, who pointed out the two sets of parallel wagon train ruts cut deep into the prairie top soil, still visible today east of the main gate leading into Peterson Field Air Force Base. These wagon wheel ruts extended from the south, now partially covered over by one of the runways for the Colorado Springs Municipal Airport. Grandpa explained that at one time the traffic became so heavy along this wagon train route that the old timers had to deploy two-way traffic to accommodate the flow of the north and south bound wagons.

Later research would reveal this route was part of the Cherokee Trail, and further to the north traversed along the same route as the Jimmy Camp Trail, a trail established in the early 1800s by James Daugherty, one of the earliest, if not the first trader to set up camp where the plains came to rest at the foot of Pikes Peak. Approximately two miles east of Peterson Field's main gate, along Highway 94, is a bridge we crossed at Jimmy Camp Creek, marking the location where just north of the highway under the shade of the large cottonwood trees, Jimmy would set up camp and light a fire with green limbs sending up smoke to signal he was open for trade with the local Indians. At one time there was a bronze plaque that marked the location of Jimmy's camp along Jimmy Camp Creek.

My second memory is of my mother pointing out the many bison wallows: shallow depressions in the earth measuring 30-40 feet in diameter created by the American bison. The bison would roll in the wet mud, causing the depressions, after a spring rain to cool off, scrape off their excess winter hair, covering themselves with thick mud to help protect from biting insects. Brought back from the edge of extinction, the American bison of today can often be seen with blackbirds riding atop their backs, pecking away in the thick thatch of hair covering the bison hump, consuming unseen quantities of insects rich in protein, an apparent mutually beneficial arrangement that had been played out across the plains no doubt many thousands of years.

Whenever I found myself walking through the tall bison grasslands in search of a wayward cow in need of her twice daily milking or running in pursuit of the usually uncooperative horse I had hoped to ride, my eyes constantly scanned the ground ahead in hopes of discovering another ancient arrowhead or stone artifact laying in the dirt that I could add to my modest arrowhead collection. Living in eastern El Paso County between the small towns of Ellicott to the southwest and Calhan to our north, I learned another important lesson: to always scan the ground ahead for the deadly rattlesnake.

As boys, my cousins and friends who lived nearby and I were taught it was our obligation to kill any rattlesnake we came across, unless in doing this put our own lives in danger. Rattlesnakes were not only a deadly menace to us and our families, but they also threatened our livestock, especially a curious young calf who often approached anything of interest nose first. We were taught how to quickly tell the difference between the diamond-shaped patterns on the back of a rattler, with a distinctively shaped tan colored rattle at the tip of its tail, from a common bullsnake, which we were sternly lectured to leave alone, unharmed, for they were our friends. We were repeatedly told by cattlemen how over a bullsnake's lifetime, they would eat hundreds of field mice and jackrabbits which burrowed holes into the ground. If a horse accidentally stepped into a gopher hole, it could cripple the horse and throw a rider. One of the saddest days for horse and rider, was when a horse with a broken leg had to be shot to put it down and out of its misery.

However, the single most important lesson that we were taught regarding why we were to leave the bullsnake alone was because they ate the dreaded rattlesnakes! Some unconfirmed estimates claimed a bullsnake would easily eat as many as 10-12 rattlesnakes a year, but exactly how anyone actually knew this statistic to be factual was never questioned. It was known that mature bullsnakes might live well past 8-10 years, consuming an impressive number of rattlesnakes during their lifetime. As young children, we were taught a very important lesson by our elders: you cannot affect one part of nature without adversely impacting another, a lesson that had been also handed down to the Ute children by their Tribal Elders for many centuries.

Reflecting back to my arrowhead hunting adventures, the rewards of my careful observations were, in addition to not being snake-bitten, spotting the occasional glint of sunlight reflecting off a small triangular piece of flint, more noticeable I learned following the rare spring rain in eastern El Paso County. Picking up my newfound treasure, I would give it a careful inspection for any flaking caused by a human hand. I learned to search the surface edges for that distinctive conchoidal striation pattern caused by skilled hands, who had long ago applied the proper pressure at the precise point, to chip away small flakes of stone, ultimately shaping the two cutting sides of the arrowhead. I would search for indications of two notches opposite the projectile point, where the stone tool had been affixed to the wooden shaft of the arrow: further evidence this stone artifact had long ago been crafted by human hand, not by an act of nature. Clutching the arrowhead tightly in hand, I would sometimes scan the surrounding terrain, allowing my mind to wander back in time, trying to reconstruct how it was this ancient projectile point came to rest at this particular site; was it shot into the air by a mounted Native American hunter or warrior, missing its intended target, perhaps a fleeting prong horned antelope or maybe a charging bison? This really was the beginning of my interested in Native Americans.

Nearly a quarter of a century after graduating from high school and moving away from our family ranch, I came across a curiously disfigured Ponderosa pine tree, its trunk bent in an unnatural position. My first discovery, of what I later confirmed was a Ute Indian Prayer Tree, was northeast of Pikes Peak in the Black Forest of northern El Paso County. I remember hiking in Fox Run Park with my daughter, Laynie, and near a well-worn trail was a strangely bent, distorted Ponderosa tree. I questioned briefly at the time what may have caused its peculiar shape, thinking it was likely human caused.

Like most other people, I did not associate the oddly shaped tree to Native Americans from long ago, nor did I suspect any spiritual or navigational purpose. What I did do was to register the location of this unusual tree mentally, identifiable by its unusual bent trunk, appearing definitely unnatural when compared to the other trees around it, potentially shaped through human intervention. I hoped that someday I might be able to return to this spot, should time ever permit, to discover the mystery that lay behind this unusually distorted old pine tree.

The first reference I remember reading about Ute Indian Prayer Trees was in a local newspaper article about the Ute Indians, *The Gazette* Sunday, July 16, 2000. I am fairly certain it was during my term as Sheriff for El Paso County, Colorado (1995-2003). I had always remained fascinated with Native American history and stone artifacts since childhood, but other interruptions of family life, work and duties of public office demanded most of my time.

Several years previous while working as a detective during my career with the Colorado Springs Police Department (1972-1995), I worked a homicide investigation with the Ute Tribal Police from the Ute Mountain Ute Reservation. On a few occasions I had also taught criminal investigations courses in Durango, Colorado, attended by several members of the Ute Tribal Police from the Southern Ute and Ute Mountain Ute Reservations. Although the subject of Ute Indian Prayer Trees never came up at the time, my limited understanding of the Ute culture and appreciation for their rich history grew through these few professional law enforcement encounters.

One important lesson I did learn was the position of importance the Ute Tribal Elder held within their tribal culture. This admirable quality became abundantly clear during one of my first investigative classes I taught near the Reservation when a dozen or more tribal police officers sat in the back of the class, arms folded across their chests, refusing to engage with the class or ask or answer any questions. It was not until their Tribal Elder finally spoke, would they start to become engaged in the class. I soon came to appreciate the status of rank, held in such high regard in most police agencies, meant little to the Ute, in comparison to the status of being the eldest, the one revered, for they held the collective wisdom of their Tribal Elders from long past.

The newspaper article on the Ute did further awaken my interest in the oddly shaped trees I had seen. The article provided a brief historical overview and as I recall, suggested these intriguing old trees had a spiritual connection for the Ute, while serving other purposes such as being an Indian trail marker. From what I read and from personal experience, my friends and I initially thought that there may only be a handful of these historically significant trees remaining in all of the Pikes Peak Region. Remarkably, more than a decade later I would discover the Pikes Peak Region to be richly covered in these historic Ute Indian Prayer Trees. I would come to learn many Trailmarker trees were hundreds of years old, and most were located along Indian trails that were perhaps thousands of years old, maybe even ten thousand years old.

The time for me to devote myself and use my investigative training toward the subject of Ute Indian Prayer Trees finally arrived when I retired in the fall of 2012. My retirement fell on Columbus Day and now was my time to go discover New Worlds, or actually in my case, to rediscover Old Worlds and to seek out others interested in researching these fascinating old trees. It was nice to realize that I wasn't alone and that I didn't have to start from scratch. Other historians, although few in number, had previously been as committed as I was to learn as much as possible from what became known to me as Ute Indian Prayer Trees.

As my field research began to expand with the help of my ever expanding circle of friends I soon confirmed, that there were far more of these richly historic trees across Colorado than I had ever thought possible to have survived. Some had been standing here for hundreds of years. What was even more exciting was the possibility these trees had helped guide our Native Americans across vast interconnected trails which were proving to be far more comprehensive than I ever could have imagined.

While traveling and hiking with friends across countless miles of trails in search of the mysteries that surround the Ute Indian Prayer Trees, I have often wondered when any of these trees may have been actually last touched by a Ute. History teaches us that the Cherokee Nation were the first Native Americans to be forced on to a reservation, from the late 1820's to 1838 in the southern state of Georgia. The Ute were the last Native Americans in the State of Colorado to be forced onto reservations.

Tragically, when the Ute were forced on to Reservations, they no longer had access to their sacred trees. The more I learned about these trees, the more important it became to be part of introducing others to the trees and reconnecting the Ute to the trees and the trees to the Ute.

I have come to share the opinion of historians who believe that the vast network of our Native American Trails once extended from the Atlantic to the Pacific Ocean and from far north into Canada all the way south, down along the Rocky Mountain Front Range connecting the Americas. All along this extensive trail system were culturally modified trees, rock cairns and rock art to serve as trail markers, navigational beacons that have not only remained a mystery, but nearly vanished from the historical record altogether. Most ancient trial researchers today suggest the Culturally Modified Trees located across the 48 states were first cultivated in the 1600's, but perhaps they originated back much further in our history.

Culturally Modified Trees in the Pikes Peak Region are but a small, yet uniquely important part of that story. My research and journey is not just about sacred trees. It is about sacred places and spiritually centered people that modified these trees, including the Ute.

To me, there will always be something mysterious, something spiritual, about walking along a quiet trail through a forest following in the ancient footsteps of the Native Americans from the distant past. Discovering an ancient Ute Indian Prayer Tree, caressing its bark and running fingers across a ligature mark embedded deep into the curvature of the trunk, is a gift from an ancient people and their Creator. Exploring an area where the bark was peeled away by a Ute Medicine Man in search of the cambium layer to heal a tribal member is evidence of an advanced culture.

I must confess to never thinking of myself as retiring to become a "tree hugger." I do, on occasion, find myself closing my eyes and wrapping my arms around the sturdy trunk of an old Ponderosa, one who stood in the Black Forest for centuries, and placing my ear along the trunk in an attempt to hear the drumbeat of a distant past, a sacred time when the Ute lived free and cultivated these sacred trees so very long ago. These trees offer undeniable proof: they were here, right here was where their tepees were nestled among the trees of the Shining Mountains.

I try to pause at every tree line that borders a grassy meadow, my eyes searching the native grasslands, wondering where the Ute may have staked out their prized Paint Ponies, built their campfires to prepare their meals, stood together as a family to gaze up at the stars that helped guide their way through the Shining Mountains. Wherever I walk with my black lab, I wonder where the Ute may have fed their loyal dogs scraps of meat or draped their bison hides over wooden racks for tanning. I search the ground for tepee rings, proof of where they positioned their lodge poles to form their shelters, carefully aligned with the opening flap facing east to catch the early morning's first sunlight, another gift from their Creator.

In learning about the original Colorado's inhabitants you will find the fascinating lives of a remarkably resilient people and discover a people whose tribal ancestors cultivated these mysterious sacred trees of the Pikes Peak Region. This journey gives the opportunity for adventure with family and friends and an opportunity to meet people whom you would never have met as you go in search of these Ute Prayer Trees.

My best hope is that this humble work somehow lends itself to enhancing the education, appreciation and preservation of perhaps the last living artifact left behind by the Native American Indians of long ago, the Ute Indian Prayer Trees of the Pikes Peak Region.

"You are the people you meet and the books you read."
—Abraham Lincoln, 16th President of the United States

Chapter 2 - Culturally Modified Trees
Tava (Pikes Peak) is sacred; the Creator has the sun rise there first.

The history and culture of the Ute Native American Indians, like many other cultures around the world, is abundantly rich in art, science and music, and as with a few other advanced cultures, the history and the culture of the Ute people also included the skillful cultivation of trees. Ute Indian Prayer Trees can be categorized as a subgroup of what are more widely known as Culturally Modified Trees (CMT), which have been found on six of the world's seven continents. Ute Prayer Trees (UPT) are CMTs that have been permanently bent, distorted, twisted, peeled or scarred by the Ute people for spiritual, medicinal, nutritional, burial or navigational purposes, long ago.

UPTs can still be found today, living artifacts from hundreds of years ago, skillfully crafted by the strong hands of the original inhabitants of what are today Colorado Rocky Mountains. We can trace early man's interactions, traditions or cultural practices with trees back to our earliest time, when man first climbed a tree for safety or used its heights for observation or stretched out across its limbs reaching for something to eat. Man's earliest interaction with trees would have altered the tree's natural configuration, modifying the shape of the tree, inadvertently or intentionally, distinguishing that specific tree apart from other trees.

When or where the cultural modification of trees first occurred will likely never be known; however, the most widely recognized CMTs are the Bonsai Trees of Japan, which are known to have originated around 200 A.D. in China. The Japanese culture cultivates Bonsai trees for aesthetic purposes perhaps, as well as a means of relaxation or meditation. Julian Velasco, the curator of the Brooklyn Botanic Garden's Bonsai collection, one of the oldest and largest Bonsai collections outside of Japan, explains, "Bonsai is horticulture, art, philosophy and even a way of life in a single tree, lovingly pruned and trained to exist in a small pot so that it reflects the majesty of the natural environment."

Perhaps, as with the Bonsai, the Ute Prayer Trees can best be described by applying Velasco's quote, and replacing the word "Bonsai" with "Ute Prayer Tree" and the word "pot" to read "space" as follows: a "Ute Prayer Tree is horticulture, art, philosophy and even a way of life in a single tree, lovingly pruned and trained to exist in a small space so that it reflects the majesty of the natural environment." In both cultures, which share many other remarkable similarities, both the Japanese and Ute People seemed to share a passion, and beauty, and transformation for their CMTs.

In Irving Howbert's book *Indians of the Pikes Peak Region,* he expressed his opinion about the Ute over a century ago, which remains consistent with most historians, "I am firmly of the opinion that these Indians, and in fact all the Indians of America, are descendants of Asiatic tribes that crossed over to this continent by way of the Bering Strait at some remote period. These tribes may; however, have been added to at various times by chance migrations from Japan, the Hawaiian and South Sea Islands. It is known that in historic times the Japanese current has thrown upon the Pacific Coast fishing-boats, laden with Japanese people, which had drifted helplessly across the Pacific Ocean. It is therefore, fair to assume that what is known to have occurred in recent times might also have frequently occurred in the remote past, and if this be so, the intermarriage of these people with the native races would undoubtedly have had a decided influence upon the tribes adjacent to the Pacific Coast."

Howbert continues to cite an article published in *The National Geographic Magazine*, of April 1910, written by a Miss Scidmore, titled "Mukden, the Manchu Home" which states, "When I saw the Viceroy and his suite at the Japanese fête at Tairen, whither he had gone to pay a state visit, I was convinced as never before of the common origin of the North American Indian and the Chinese or Manchu Tartars. There before me might as well have been Red Cloud, Sitting Bull, and Rain-in-the-Face, dressed in blue satin blankets, thick-soled moccasins, and squat war-bonnets with single bunches of feathers shooting back from the crown. Manchu eyes, Tartar cheek-bones, and Mongol jaws were combined in countenances that any Sioux chief would recognize as a brother."

Howbert then continues in his own words, and speaking from first-hand experience, "The Ute Indians were well-built, but not nearly as tall as the Sioux, Cheyenne, Arapahoe or any of the tribes of the plains. Their type of countenance was substantially the same that of all American Indians. They were distinctly mountain Indians, and that they should have been a shorter race than those of the plains to the east is peculiar…Might not this have been the result of an infusion of Japanese blood in the early days of the Shoshones when their numbers were small? And possibly from the same source came the unusual ability of the Ute in warfare… as they were remarkably good fighters and more than able to hold their own against equal numbers."

In North America, there have been CMTs found in nearly all of the contiguous 48 states, as well as in forests in Alaska and across Canada. A publication titled *Culturally Modified Trees of British Columbia, A Handbook for the Identification and Recording of Culturally Modified Trees*, prepared by the Archaeology Branch B.C. Ministry of Small Business, Tourism and Culture for the Resource Inventory Committee (March 2001 Version 2.0) provides the Definition of CMT as, "CMT is a tree that has been altered by aboriginal people as part of their traditional use of the forest. Non-aboriginal people also have altered trees, and it is sometimes difficult to determine if an alteration (modification) is of aboriginal or non-aboriginal origin. There are no reasons why the term "CMT" could not be applied to a tree altered by non-aboriginal people. However, the term is commonly used to refer to trees modified by aboriginal people in the course of traditional tree utilization, and is used as such in this handbook."

This handbook went on to divide CMTs in British Columbia into three main groups or classes; Bark-Stripped Tree, Aboriginally-Logged Tree, and Other Modified Tree, then each of these classes were further subdivided into a number of related types (e.g., Pitch Collection Tree, Sap Collection Tree, and Canoe Tree). The handbook provides a good description of key terms with a glossary at the back of the publication and cataloged a number of CMT Toolmarks (i.e., bone chisels, stone handmauls, and wedges made of wood, bone or antler), and even describes fire being used as a tool (e.g., to hollow out canoes).

This Canadian CMT handbook also illustrated how to determine the date the tree was modified, and described how to determine the age of a tree by comparatively dating similar unmodified trees located within the same stand of trees, as the CMT. The handbook suggests that the "presence of clusters of scarred trees increases the chance the bark scars are cultural" and references that the oldest CMT found in British Columbia at the time the handbook was published, was an "internal scar, created by bark stripping in 1186 A.D." although it suggests that most known CMTs were believed to have been modified in the 1700 and 1800's. This seems consistent with CMTs discovered in the U.S., as well as most of the UPTs located in the Pikes Peak Region.

CMTs in British Columbia are protected by Canadian law and the handbook provides the warning, "People encountering CMTs are encouraged to make a record of the findings. However, care should be taken to not damage, move or in any other way impact a CMT or CMT site which may be protected under provisions of the Heritage Conservation Act without the appropriate permit (see section on CMT protection). This includes the coring of trees for dating purposes. Impacts may affect the physical, cultural and historical integrity of a CMT or CMT site." With so many UPT on private property, one would hope that the same respect for these trees would be shown.

In the United States, there has been some groundbreaking work done by a small group of retirees in Georgia who recently celebrated their tenth year anniversary as a not-for-profit organization. They refer to themselves as the Georgia Mountain Stewards and are led by Don Wells along with his wife Diane, who published an outstanding CMT reference book, *The Mystery of the Trees, Native American Markers of a Cultural Way of Life that May Soon Be Gone.* Don also publishes a quarterly Trail Trees Newsletter and along with his dedicated team has filmed a television documentary focused on Native American Trailmarker Trees. The Georgia Mountain Stewarts have now located Trailmarker CMTs in over 40 states, including Colorado.

The research being conducted by Don and his team presents a very compelling case for the existence of a once vast Native American Trail system that extended across the North American

Continent, connecting the Native American peoples from the Atlantic to the Pacific Oceans, from Canada to northern Mexico, including the indigenous people across the Rocky Mountain Front Range of what is today the Pikes Peak Region of Colorado.

Native Trail Trees or Trailmarker Trees are occasionally found along a water way and might give a tribal member a bearing along the bank where to cross a river or creek, similar to perhaps a street sign you might see today letting a pedestrian know where it is safe to cross a street. Don and Diane Wells' book *Mystery of the Trees* displays several nice trail maps and show some very intriguing CMT photography. Don was interviewed by Lynn Armitage for an article that appeared in *This Week from Indian Country Today*, May 1, 2013. In the article, Don was quoted as saying, "We started finding Indian trails that we could document from historical maps…and we were locating oddly shaped trees on these trails that had been bent by Indians."

During this same interview, Lynn Armitage asked Don Wells, "What do these trees tell you about Native Americans from many years ago?" Don replied, "That they were very smart and very close to the earth. They could name every plant and know what they could use it for. They knew the trees and could use them to their benefit. That's why pioneers hired Indians as guides – that's the only way they could get around. These people knew a lot and they were very smart and very knowledgeable. Unfortunately, a lot of knowledge is gone now because we lost the elders."

Like Lynn Armitage, I had many questions about the Ute Indian Prayer Trees such as; "How long ago did Ute live in what is today El Paso County, Colorado? Why did the Ute modify trees and what cultural purposes might the practice of tree cultivation serve? Are they part of a larger navigational system of Trailmarker Trees? How old are these living tributes to the Ute Indians? How many of these historical trees have survived until today in the Pikes Peak Region?" These are questions that I attempt to address, but with no definitive agreed upon source or recognized publication by the Ute Nation, much of what appears here in this text is best guess or what is generally accepted, but admittedly, not everyone is in concurrence on all topics.

Ute Indian Prayer Trees may again be referred to by many different names such as Ute Sacred Trees or Ute Cultural Trees or Ute Peeled Trees and for our publication purposes as Ute Prayer Trees (UPT). CMTs were cultivated by many Native American Tribes including the Ute, the Cherokee and Cheyenne, but UPT were only cultivated by the Ute and may be somewhat unique in purpose to their Tribe. Whether the UPT was intended for navigation, medicinal, nutritional or burial purposes, the Ute tree cultivation practices and traditions were interwoven with their spiritual beliefs, and prayers offered to the Creator during each of their tree modification practices.

It is perhaps this spiritual link that separate UPTs from most other CMTs or even other Native American Trailmarker Trees which appear to have a more utilitarian purpose. In addition to serving as a navigational tool, many Ute believe these trees have a spiritual connection, a sacred bond that exists to this day, between the Ute People, their Prayer Trees and their Creator. The

Ute believe that all living things have a spirit, which links the Ute spiritually to the trees, eagles, bears, horses, grass, dogs, and other non-Native people. The Ute believe all living things in nature were, and are intertwined and when they pray around a Prayer Tree it carries their prayers up the tree towards the Creator where their prayers become intermingled with prayers of their ancestors who prayed around that particular Prayer Tree. When Ute descendants who follow in their ancestor's footsteps gather to pray around their Ute Prayer Trees their prayers are united with the prayers of all generations. When the breeze blows the Ute feel the Ponderosa's pine needles gently released their prayers which are carried by the wind across the land for the next eight hundred years (the lifespan of a Ponderosa Pine tree).

The Ute believed in one Creator, to whom they prayed for specific purposes, such as a successful hunt or courage in battle or the healing or passing of a loved one who has "walked on." It is believed that all major Ute tribal activities were associated with prayer and oftentimes memorialized by the modification of a UPT. Some UPTs were used in the marking of a specific trail leading to a favorite hunting ground or where a significant battle took place or where a loved one may have died or been buried. Since prayer seems to have been associated with each type of tree ceremony the term Ute Indian Prayer Tree or Ute Prayer Tree (UPT) seems to be an appropriate name generally applied to all the various types of Ute Prayer Trees (burial, medicine, message, trailmarker, etc.).

The UPTs found today in the Pikes Peak Region are primarily Ponderosa Pine and were intentionally selected and carefully cultivated to create their distinct shape or distorted trunk or twisted branches. Depending upon the purpose or altitude, the Juniper or Cedar or higher up Bristlecone Pines, were sometimes modified by the Ute, but most UPT seem to be found between 6,000 and 9,000 feet above sea level, known as the Montane Zone, and are typically Ponderosa Pines. The direction the tree points or leans is not random, but were purposely trained to point towards a specific direction: to help tell a story or mark a trail for navigation or possibly both.

In researching UPTs I have enjoyed several visits to the National Museum of the American Indian (NMAI), in Washington D.C. and the Denver Museum of Nature and Science. I have also been privileged to participate in a personal behind-the-scenes tour of their magnificent collections of Native American artifacts, including many flint Clovis Projectile Points estimated to be circa 10,000 B.C and Folsom Points found throughout Colorado. Tours of the Ute Museum in Montrose Colorado and the Southern Ute Cultural Center and Museum in Ignacio Colorado also house many outstanding Native American and Ute artifacts; however there are no exhibits or displays that showcase the advanced culture demonstrated through the tree modification practices of the Native American and there is almost nothing that could be found in print at any of these world-class museum collections or libraries or gift shops about Ute Prayer Trees.

On the cover of the *Black Forest Regional Park, Forestry and Noxious Weed Management*

Plan, a project funded and published in 2010 by the El Paso County (Colorado) Parks, stands a magnificent UPT that sadly may have been lost during the Black Forest Fire of 2013. This report was authored by Rebecca G. Wegner, Consulting Forester with Mountain High Tree, Inc., a tree care and consulting company in Colorado Springs that had been contracted to conduct the "research for the project, collect and interpret the data, and write, format and compile the final assessment of the document." Rebecca Wegner holds a Bachelor of Science Degree in Natural Resource Management from Colorado State University in Fort Collins, Colorado. She is a member of the American Society of Consulting Arborists, Registered Consulting Arborists and Certified Arborist, with the International Society of Arboriculture. Page three of the project report explains the cover photograph as follows:

The photograph on the front cover is of a uniquely structured Ponderosa pine in Black Forest Regional Park. The tree likely was never cut because of the fire scar on the trunk and its contorted form. It is possible that this tree was modified by Native Americans. These are called culturally modified trees (CMT). There are hundreds of Ponderosa pines in the Pikes Peak region and other areas of Colorado that have been identified as a CMT. Many were likely tied down and bent by the Ute Indians, who lived in mountainous areas of Colorado for centuries.

These bent trees usually curve horizontally near the base for a few feet then head toward the sky again, creating unusual trunk formations. Ute oral history suggests that they would use yucca rope to tie down young saplings. Also, they were said to be part of a prayer ritual perhaps to direct prayers to nearby sacred sites such as springs or mountains or to pray on special places. The natives also peeled large sections of bark off Ponderosa pines with stones, axes and sticks for the nutritious inner layer. The cambium (inner bark) could be used for medicine, food, and to make tea. The bark was good for making trays and cradle boards and the pitch for adhesives and waterproofing blankets. Many of these trees have been found on mountain passes and historic trails.

Ute Indian CMTs can be found all across the Pikes Peak Region but perhaps no more densely clustered than in the Black Forest of northern El Paso County. It is believed the thickest existing grouping of UPTs to be observed today is along the many trails in the Fox Run Regional Park. Subsequent trips into the burn area of the Black Forest confirm we lost many old UPTs, but one important point becomes self-evident; the Black Forest has become densely overpopulated with trees and fire mitigation efforts are far more effective then fire suppression. Conversations with arborists around the state confirm this point and also add that the cost of mitigation when compared to the cost of fighting a forest fire is money well spent.

Mitigation effort to protect UPTs and thin areas that are overpopulated with trees is a necessity. In early El Paso County lumber was needed to build towns as settlers increased. Sawmills appeared in the area and the Ute began to lose continuous access to their sacred trees and sacred locations. Conservation of trees was not considered during this time as it is today. It is fortunate that many UPTs, due to their distorted and bent modifications, would not be good for building purposes, saving them from being destroyed for lumber. In Judy von Ahlefeldt's book *Thunder, Sun and Snow, A History of Colorado's Black Forest*, she provides an excellent chronology of the burgeoning lumber business. The first lumber mill was built on Black Squirrel Creek, in the Black Forest Area. By the 1880s there were over a dozen sawmills located in the Black Forest.

The Ute were the only Native American Indian Tribe with a sustained presence in the Pikes Peak Region known to have cultivated Prayer Trees. This may be partially attributed to the belief that other tribes, including the Comanche, Arapahoe, Cheyenne and to a lesser extent the Sioux, migrated into the Pikes Peak Region from elsewhere, usually from the east or northeast after being displaced from their ancestral homelands by European settlers. One fact remains, the Ute Indians have been in the Pikes Peak Region for hundreds, perhaps even thousands of years, and many of these CMTs are hundreds of years old.

The broad migratory hunting ranges most Native American Indian tribes would travel may not have permitted a sustained presence in the Pikes Peak Region, for they often covered distances that today would encompass several connecting states. Unlike other tribes, the Ute primarily lived in what they referred to as the Shining Mountains, the areas of what is today northern New Mexico, eastern Utah, southern Wyoming and most of Colorado, extending across the Rocky Mountains and as far east as the Kansas state line. Several Ute bands including the Tabeguache, Capote, and Mouache, often remained within sight of their Shining Mountains, the Spanish Peaks or the San Juan or Sangre de Cristo Ranges or their most sacred mountain, Tava.

Archaeological evidence consisting of Clovis Projectile Points, arrowheads and spear points found within the original boundaries of El Paso County, which today encompasses all of El Paso and Tellers counties, have been dated to as early as 10,000 to 13,000 B.C. These two counties are connected by the Ute Pass, one of the oldest Native American Indian Trails in North America, and Ute Prayer Trees can still be found today lining this trail. Ancient artifacts that have been unearthed directly northwest and northeast of Pikes Peak establish human activity that may predate the Great Egyptian Pyramid by 10,000 years. Some historians believe the Ute Indians may have migrated to the Pikes Peak Region from the Pacific Northwest after crossing the Bering land bridge long ago.

The Ute Elders say it's the other way around. Their oral history tells them they have been here since the beginning of time and other tribes descend from them. The Elders point to the fact that they, as a people, do not have a migration story unlike almost all other Native American Tribes, many of whom claim to have migrated across the Bering Strait at the end of the last ice age, approximately 14,000 years ago. Clearly, someone was here in the Pikes Peak Region thousands of years ago. If not the Ute, then who was here? And where did the Ute go? And where did the Ute come from? The time of pre-history before a written record was made suggests the Ute were present in the Shining Mountains, as they claim, but undeniably at the time history was first recorded, especially by the Spanish, the confirmed presence of the Ute was absolutely undeniable.

The Spanish called the Ute, Yutahs, the "forever-ago people." The Ute say they have always been called the Ute and point to their rich oral history which reinforces their beliefs that they have been here since the beginning of time. In the absence of hard evidence it seems reasonable to accept oral history or tribal stories, as potentially having some kernel of truth. The Southern Ute Cultural Center and Museum (SUCCM) located on the Southern Ute Reservation in Ignacio, Colorado, claims to have DNA studies which confirm their existence in this region going back 14,000 years, which translates to approximately 560 generations. One can see why they might believe that, for them, is the beginning of time.

Establishing who the indigenous people were and establishing which Native people had a sustained presence in the Pikes Peak Region prior to the pioneers, settlers or miners of the 1860-1880s, is an important key to unlocking the mystery as to who cultivated these trees. There is no doubt other tribes visited the Pikes Peak Region on a regular basis, many intent on raiding the Ute, including the Comanche, Cheyenne and Arapahoe.

The fact that the growth of many of the more complex UPTs such as the Prophecy or Intertwined Trees would have certainly required a sustained presence of many years, perhaps requiring generations to cultivate the fascinating results of what we observe today. Only the Ute continually surface as the oldest most continuous and last remaining Native American People of the Pikes Peak Region.

Trailmarker Bookends: These two Ute Trailmarker Trees are standing on a lot on the northeast corner of the intersection of Roller Coaster Road and Trumpeter Lane near Kings Deer, in northern El Paso County, Colorado. Trailmarker Trees are listed as the first of five types or varieties of Ute Prayer Trees as they appear to be the most common. They are occasionally found in pairs and when found as a pair they usually lean at parallel angles pointing in the same direction. These two trees display evidence of ligature marks around the bark at the inside of the bend where they were staked to the ground and the second tree in the background displays the classical peeled bark pattern (bark cut at the top, peeled down the trunk and torn away at the bottom). Interestingly enough, peeled bark patterns are found on Ute Prayer Trees (UPT) in less than half the time and when found in pairs, as with these two, usually only one Trailmarker displays the classical peeled bark pattern generally attributed to the Ute Medicine Man (or Medicine Woman). These two Trailmarkers are pointing southeast towards the Arkansas/Platte Divide (Palmer Divide) where the Cherokee Trail crosses to the north through the Black Forest in El Paso County. The Cherokee Trail connected the old Santa Fe Trail which followed the Arkansas River, to the Oregon California Trail, then crossed the South Platte River near today's Auraria Campus in downtown Denver, Colorado.

La Foret Medicine Tree: This Ute Medicine Tree displays the classical peeled bark pattern of the Ute Medicine Man and is located along the northern edge of a beautiful grassy meadow directly northwest of the Taylor Memorial Chapel in La Foret, El Paso County, Colorado. The tree is located between Burgess Creek to the south and Kettle Creek to the north. It is slightly bent and points to the north. This tree displays the traditional peeled bark signature pattern of the Ute Medicine Man or Medicine Woman starting with the ceremonial first cut at the top with an ax then the bark is peeled away from the tree and torn off at the bottom. What is unusual about this peeled bark pattern is its length. The pattern begins about 10-12 feet above the ground then extends downward to ground level evidence that the bark skillfully removed in one piece in such a way as to not kill the tree. To begin this peeled bark pattern so high above ground level suggests the Ute Medicine Man would have had to standing on something, a scaffolding of some type or perhaps standing on his horse. Two stone or wooden wedges were used by the Medicine Man and driven downward between the outer bark and the inner hardwood to extract the mineral laden cambium layer. The outer bark was also used for various utilitarian purposes which may have included using the outer bark for food preparation or as serving trays or cradleboards.

Inset: **Medicine Tree (Ute Ceremonial Tree)** located on the Three Eagles Ranch in southern Douglas County, Colorado. Ute Medicine Trees are often used for dual purposes, such as a Burial Tree where bark may be peeled away for ceremonial purposes related to the deceased love one. The scar shown is part of a tree believed to have been used as a Ute Ceremonial Tree. This tree has been estimated to be well over three hundred years old. Thick bark has grown around the edges of the peeled bark scar evidence that the scar was caused long ago. Inside the cut scar is a scorched burn area, possibly associated with a Ute ceremony. Just above the peeled bark scar is a deformation of the tree called a burl, which results when a tree undergoes some form of distress, such as an injury, virus or fungus. This old burl is believed to have been man-caused and they are occasionally found in association with other ceremonial peeled bark patterns. As with all CMT examinations it is important to take the entire topography into consideration when assessing a possible candidate UPT. For example; the Three Eagles Ranch is situated on the high ground between the Ute Pass and the grassy high plains where buffalo hunts occurred. Found on a bluff on the Ranch property were multiple rock hand carved water basins with connecting downhill troughs and several smooth stone manos consistent with those that would have been used by the Ute women for food preparation.

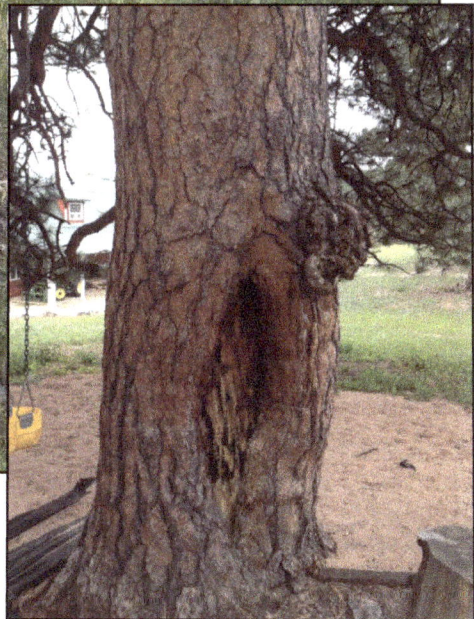

Burial Tree: The Burial Tree is the third variety or type of Ute Prayer Trees. The Ute Burial Tree pictured is one of the largest Ute Burial Trees found in Colorado. It is located on private property just inside the gated entrance to the High Forest Ranch, on Highway 83, in El Paso County, Colorado. Ute Burial Trees are identifiable by two distinct 90° bends forming right angles. The Ute believe all life comes from Mother Earth and we all walk across the earth in life, represented by the first 90° bend followed by the trunk running parallel to the ground. At the end of life, the Ute believe, we all ascend up to the Creator, represented by the second 90° bend extending upward. This Ute Prayer Tree also carries the classic Ute peeled bark pattern along the top of the trunk between the two bends, which displays the traditional ceremonial first cut towards the top of the tree, downward peel and torn bark pattern towards its base. The direction a Ute Burial Tree points is representative of the life of the Ute being honored and traditionally points to where that person died or was buried or may have been born. Some Ute Burial Trees have been found in the Black Forest with longer horizontal trunks (6-8 feet in length) and a few with relatively short horizontal trunks (the shortest was only 14 inches) which may be an indication of the length of that tribal member's lifespan. The property where this tree is located was at one time part of the Shamrock Ranch until the property was subdivided and sold. The direction this tree points is towards the south where much of the Shamrock Ranch property still remains intact. Further to the south, also on private property, are three large man-made mounds constructed of stacked rock and covered with dirt. These mounds are located in a protected area, along an old foot trail near the curve of a small creek found just downstream and below an artesian spring located on the Shamrock Ranch near what use to be a stagecoach stop in the 1800's.

Story Tree: Ute Story or Message Trees are the fourth variety of Ute Prayer Trees and are believed to have been a form of communication within the tribe or possibly between two or more different tribes. As with other Ute Prayer Tree types they may serve dual purposes; such as being directional, like the Trailmarker Trees, while communicating a message, such as where to find water. It appears that some messages may have been intended to serve as short term means of communication, including those images carved on the bark of an Aspen Tree which have a shorter lifespan than most pine trees. Other Message Trees may have been used like street signs are today and many seem to have pointed towards sources of fresh water. The Cherokee Indians used a similar method of modify a tree to point to where springs could be located and the number of branches or secondary trunks may indicate the number of springs that could be found ahead. The Message Tree in this photo may have pointed to where four or possibly five artesian springs could be located in the Black Forest. Other more complex story trees would have taken years, perhaps even generations to cultivate. The more intricate designs may have been used by the Ute Elders to help pass their oral history from one generation to the next. This Message Tree is located in Fox Run Regional Park, on the north side of Baptist Road, west of Roller Coaster Road, in El Paso County, Colorado.

La Foret Grandfather Tree: This is believed to be one of the oldest Ute Prayer Trees in the Black Forest. This Trailmarker Tree displays the classical peeled bark pattern of the Ute Medicine Man (the missing bark area is partially visible in the photo on the lower right side of the trunk ending at about three feet above ground level). The tree also displays the small protruding primary trunk or spur and partial ligature marks are observable on the inside of its one 30° bend approximately 18 feet above the ground. It also shows evidence of a man caused horizontal six inch cut about a foot above the ground which is believed to have been used to collect pine pitch collected for various spiritual, medicinal, nutritional and utilitarian purposes. This tree has been visited by the Ute now returning to the Black Forest to reconnect with their sacred Ute Prayer Trees and has been the site of several recent sacred tree ceremonies. Many educational Ute Prayer Tree Tours begin at this tree which then traverses west around and behind the Taylor Chapel, along the right bank of Burgess Creek then returns to the Chapel. In the spring this half mile route meanders through a beautiful meadow accented with deep gamma grass and wildflowers. Near the end of the walk a Ute Medicine Tree can be inspected. The Grandfather Tree points towards Tava (Pikes Peak) and is located just north of Burgess Creek 100 yards east the Taylor Memorial Chapel, on La Foret property, in El Paso County, Colorado.

La Foret Ute Cat Face Tree: Cat Faces are a particularly intriguing variety of sacred Ute Message or Story Trees and were created when the Ute peeled away a portion of the tree bark then leaned a piece of burning wood from their campfire against the exposed hard wood of the Ponderosa Pine tree. The three dimensional images are not carved, but are what remains when the wood around the faces are burned away. The Ute believe that all trees have a spirit and if the Creator chose he may reveal to them the spirit of the tree which became visible in the burn scar after the tree ceremony is performed. The peeled bark was typically peeled from the tree in the shape of a triangle or rectangle and is typically located between 2-6 feet above the ground. The Ute observed that the most common image or scar revealed following the sacred tree ceremony resembled what the Ute called a Cat Face (commonly known today as a cougar, puma or mountain lion). Other animal faces have been found, including what resembles a bison, elk and a bear. On one occasion, when using the facial recognition capability of a smart phone, the face of a helmeted conquistador appeared (note: although not required, an active imagination is helpful when identifying Cat Faces). A two page reference was found in the archives in the basement of the Southern Ute Cultural Center and Museum (SUCCM), which cited interviews from two Ute Tribal Elders discussing how Cat Faces were formed and what they meant. One written narrative described how the Cat Face is generally found facing the upslope side of a hill, which does seem consistent with the handful of Cat Faces that have been located to date. Cat Faces are rare; however when discovered they are often found in small clusters which may suggest that not all Ute bands or families adopted this specific tree ceremonial practice. This tree is located along the right bank of Burgess Creek, on La Foret, directly west of the Taylor Chapel, in the Black Forest, El Paso County, Colorado.

Cedar Burial Tree: This large Cedar Tree is located on private property in the Black Forest of northern El Paso County, Colorado. Of significance is the fact that Cedar Trees are not indigenous to the Black Forest and as of this publication only two other Cedar Trees have been found in the Black Forest. Further, Cedar Trees are either male or female and both are required to populate other trees. Therefore this tree had to have been intentionally planted. The location a Cedar tree was planted is of significance for its location in a remote area along a trail (visible in the background behind this tree). This trail runs east to west across this property and parallels a creek which leads across this property to where a traditional Ute Burial Tree with the two 90° bends was discovered a few hundred yards to the west. Between these two types of Ute Burial Trees four small circular mounds were discovered. When sharing this photo with a Southern Ute Tribal Elder he did confirm that this tree would have been planted by "our people" as they were the only Native American tribes that he was aware of that would have planted the seeds of the Cedar Tree to mark a sacred ceremonial site. This possible burial site was pointed out to the property owner; however the mounds were respected as a likely sacred Native American site and were not disturbed.

Chapter 3 - Ute Indian Prayer Tree Types
Morning's first light is a gift from the Creator; use each of his gifts wisely.

There is no single definitive source to describe each specific type or variety, of Ute Indian Prayer Tree. If there were I believe it should come from the Ute. It is generally accepted that there are likely five (5) types of Ute Indian Prayer Trees cultivated in the Pikes Peak Region; however, there is not a consensus on what those varieties are or even the names that should be used for each type. There are also sub-groups or sub-types of trees that were modified by the Ute for cultural or utilitarian purposes such as the extraction of Bristlecone (Pine) tree pitch to be mixed with beeswax to form glue used to attach an arrowhead to the wooden arrow shaft.

All trees modified by the Ute were sacred and prayers to recognize the tree's consent and permission in the modification were made along with gratitude to the Creator, according to Ute Elders that I have met. Therefore, even though some researchers list Prayer Trees as a type of Culturally Modified Trees, I have called all CMTs modified by the Ute as Ute Prayer Trees and then categorize types under UPTs.

What complicates the subject of identifying or naming each of the UPT types even further, in addition to a lack of any written record from the Ute Nation concerning what they recognize as their sacred trees, is the fact that many of the tree categories often overlap. It is not uncommon for a Trailmarker Tree or a Burial Tree to exhibit a distinct peeled bark pattern where the Medicine Man or Medicine Woman, may have peeled away a portion of the outer bark to extract the tree's cambium layer for medicinal or nutritional purposes. Without a written language or a representative of the Ute Nation standing before a UPT explaining their cultural tree modification practices, examining or explaining the distinctions between one UPT variety and another is certainly more of an art than science, but one has to start somewhere.

Although naming and categorizing differs with those researching these trees, it is important to objectively examine all available research to help in the understanding. One additional source would be the Pikes Peak Historical Society and an article on their website by Celinda Kaelin. This site has photographs and descriptions of CMT attributed to the Ute found in Teller County and although we differ on some types, both references will help in identification of these trees.

For the purposes of this publication a distinction is being drawn to identify UPT that have had a major degree of modification from their original natural form or configuration caused by ancient (not modern) human intervention, usually being tied or staked down. Major degrees of modification would include those trees exhibiting a permanent structural change or alteration in the direction the tree would have grown naturally, caused by human intervention such as being tied or staked down.

Minor degrees of human intervention such as those trees with evidence of peeled bark or cuts in the bark for pitch collection without causing the tree to alter its natural direction when seeking sunlight, will be discussed as a sub-variety, rather than a separate type of UPT.

Most of the UPTs that can still be found in northern El Paso County, Colorado, are of the Pinus Ponderosa, commonly known as Ponderosa Pines or Ponderosas. These trees are distinguishable by their long green pine needles, a dark or depending upon their age, sometimes cinnamon colored bark and large brown pine cones (which contain the seeds). These UPTs can grow to be very large and very old; some may live to be 800 years old. The tallest known Ponderosa Trees along the Palmer Divide of northern El Paso County are over 100 feet tall and several have been measured to be over 10 feet in circumference (the current record holder is absolutely huge: with a circumference measuring 11 feet - 7 inches!).

Listed in a descending order of frequency in which they have been found still growing in the Pikes Peak Region, are many CMTs believed to be attributed to the Ute (Ute Prayer Trees). These trees generally have been accepted as belonging to one of these five classifications or major types:

1. Trailmarker Trees
2. Medicine Trees
3. Burial Trees
4. Story Trees
5. Prophecy Trees

Trailmarker Tree

The first classification of the five UPT categories appears to be the most common type of UPT, the Trailmarker Tree. These trees are still observable today in large numbers across much of the Pikes Peak Region. They can be identified by closely examining the bark of a Ponderosa Pine Trees often found with one distinctive 30 degree bend to the trunk before extending upward. The most identifiable characteristic of the Trailmarker Tree is the permanent angular bend of the trunk and a scarring or horizontal disfigurement of the bark at the point of the bend where a ligature had been wrapped around the tree when it was a sapling and bent over to stake it to the ground, always pointing towards some geographical or navigational reference point (e.g., trail, stream, mountain pass).

UPTs that serve as Trailmarker Trees can usually be identified by what looks like a dead limb that grew outward near its distinctive upward bend; however this limb is actually what remains of the primary tree trunk which had withered and died away. The close inspection of the tree's bark at the point along the inside of the Ute modified bend in the tree often reveals a permanent scarring, constriction and/or discoloration of the bark caused by the ligature device that had been tied around the tree when it was much younger and more pliable. This modification often caused a secondary branch, known to horticulturists as a leader, to grow upright off the tree's main trunk, leaving the primary branch to atrophy and wither away. The Ute believe their prayers contained within the Prayer Tree, to reach skyward toward the Creator.

Examination of the trunk or branches located nearest the point of the outside of the bend may help to make an assessment to the direction the tree points, often to another UPT or geographical location. This examination often provides further evidence of ancient human intervention such as another UPT, a firepit, ancient trail or sacred site. The direction the Trailmarker Tree is pointing is not random, but a deliberately chosen direction, trained to point towards something: Pikes Peak, a trailhead, a spring, a mountain pass, game trail or possibly leading to a burial mound.

The release of the Prayer Tree from being staked down may have been deliberate once the thirty or ninety degree bend or bends had been achieved or perhaps more likely the ligature device simply wore away after several growth seasons. I have not seen a Prayer Tree that has the ligature device still intact. Only the distinctive disfigurement around the bark has been observed suggesting the ligature was likely made of natural fiber and was cut, removed or worn away with time.

Heliotropic or heliotropism is the scientific term for a tree or a plant naturally wanting to grow straight upright to seek the direction of the sunlight. The term is derived from the Ancient Greeks who studied those plants that moved in the direction of the sun, a property they referred to as "heliotropium" meaning "sun turn." The Ute, along with other Native American Tribes, applied this principle in allowing nature to help shape or bend or turn the tree trunk or limbs, toward a specific, meaningful direction over time. This alternation was not done without some level of arboricultural skill and practice with some degree of trial and error and with the Ute, prayer.

The Ute were also aware that trees grew upward from the treetop towards the sun, not from the ground. For example, if a person who is fifteen years of age were to carve their initials in a tree at eye-level and returned to that same tree when he were sixty five, the initials would still be at the same height as when the initials were first carved into the tree a half century earlier. When attempting to reconstruct where and how the tree was staked down, this dead limb, trunk or spur can provide an important clue as to the maximum diameter and likely where the top or highest point of the tree may have been at the time it was staked to the ground.

The vast majority of UPT Trailmarker Trees were definitely modified while the person stood upon the ground; however in a few rare instances, it appears the person could have been mounted on horseback or may have had to climb the tree or built scaffolding. Trailmarker Trees are often found in pairs perhaps to ensure the survival of at least one or to make sure they are not overlooked by someone approaching from a different direction. When you find one Trailmarker Tree, it pays dividends to search the immediate area for another.

Medicine Tree

The second classification of the Ute Indian Prayer Tree is the Ute Medicine Tree. It is identifiable by the distinctive scarred bark which was deliberately peeled away from the tree trunk by a Ute Medicine Man. The pattern by which the bark was removed is very recognizable and appears to have been always scraped or peeled from the top down to the bottom and removed in one large piece or section. The top of the peeled bark section often displays a sharp angled strike caused by a stone or metal tool such as a hatchet, swung across the tree in an upward direction, thought to have been done by a Medicine Man, causing a split in the bark with an upward direction (usually pointing to the 1 o'clock position) and measuring several inches in width.

The Cheyenne Indians referred to this upwardly angled strike as a ceremonial "first strike" often accomplished by a Cheyenne woman representing the sacred White Maiden Buffalo; however it is not known if the Ute had a similar ceremony. It is known the Ute and the Cheyenne were well acquainted with one another, often through combat, and through inner-tribal trade, but it is not known if this ceremonial first strike of the tree bark is transferable from one tribe to the next. What is consistent is the pattern of the bark removal, including the manner and location of the first strike where the bark is peeled and how the bottom of the pattern is always torn away from the tree. This pattern has been observed by others, along with myself, across the Pikes Peak Region and as far north as East Vail, at the base of Gore Pass.

On the Southern Ute Indian Tribe homepage is a link to the History of the Southern Ute which describes the various plants and berries the Ute would use for medicinal or nutritional purposes.

The inner bark of the tree is very nutritious and was yet another food source for the people. The Ute harvested the inner bark of the Ponderosa pine for making healing compresses, tea and for healing. The scarred Ponderosa trees are still visible in Colorado forests. The healing trees are evidence of the Ute early presence in the land and their close relationship to the ecosystem.

When the Ute people were forcibly placed (on) reservations they could no longer travel on their familiar trails, to gather or hunt for food. As more and more elders pass they take traditional knowledge about plants and their uses with them. In the past the Ute vocabulary included many words and their uses for plants. Unfortunately, these ancient words have been lost.

Fortunately, many of the Ute Prayer Trees do survive today and can be studied, and some of the Ute Elders still remember hearing about the uses of the trees from their grandparents. One of the primary outcomes of this CMT/UPT research project is to help ensure that this piece of Ute culture and history does not drop off from the historical record altogether especially with the passing of each generation of Ute Tribal Elders.

When examining this repeatable striking pattern, the split is located on the upper part of the bark and measures 3-5 inches in length, depending upon the diameter of the tree trunk and the left side of this cut is almost always lower than the right side of the cut. This initial strike which splits the bark down to the hard wood underneath allowed the Ute Medicine Man to drive two or more stone or wooden wedges downward between the outer bark and the tree's inner hard wood separating the bark from the wood. Again the bark is consistently peeled away from the tree at an area that would have been the most easily accessible to the Medicine Man. Other UPT class characteristics that can be examined, such as a bend, spur or evidence of ligature marks should be present in order to determine with some degree of certainty a tree may be a Ute Indian Medicine Tree.

Medicine Trees are not uncommon and are typically found tightly clustered in grouping that includes other varieties of Ute Prayer Trees. Some Trailmarker Trees also contain peeled bark, thus the tree could be classified in both categories. Trailmarker Trees that do not contain peeled bark could be due to the particular band that cultivated the tree not having a Medicine Man present, or if the need for the healing or nutritional powers of the inner bark was not needed when the tree was modified.

The surface area of where the bark has been removed can vary from extending just a few inches to several feet in length and is almost always found along the uppermost surface of the tree trunk or along the upper surfaces of a limb or sometimes both. This removal pattern is distinct in that the lower portion of the bark is tapered downward, where the upper or top area displays a very distinct sharp cut extending in an upwards angle that sometimes gives a "V" or "U" shape pointing down the tree trunk.

Some trees have been observed with the bark removed twenty or more feet above the ground indicating the Medicine Man chose that location for a reason and must have been an accomplished climber in good physical condition. A few UPTs appear to have had their lower limbs cut away leaving a branch extending outward from the tree measuring 5-8 inches in length, giving the appearance these trimmed branches may have been used for handholds or footholds for climbing. One tree in the Black Forest was found with its branches trimmed almost the entire length of the tree and leaning against another tree with a peeled bark pattern where the two trees met, suggesting some Ute may have used the first tree as a ladder.

During the winter of 1868-1869, John Wesley Powell, geologist and explorer of the American West, spent several months with the Ute Indians on the White River in the northwest Colorado Territory (today the state of Colorado). In his journal, Powell wrote of witnessing the Ute

Medicine Man climbing trees to remove the bark to harvest what he called a "mucilaginous substance" known technically as the "cambium layer" found inside the tree between the hard wood inside and the outer bark. Another observation Powell recorded was how the Medicine Man would leave an area between two locations where he removed bark in order not to cause the tree to die by removing too large of a continuous area of bark. The surface areas observed are generally less than 20% of the circumference area and never removed all the way around the tree as this would cause the tree to die. Powell describe how this substance was used as a food source, but it was also used for medicinal purposes, and the outer bark was often used as a cradle board (Native American Indians waste very little).

Burial Tree

The third classification of UPT we will recognize is the Ute Indian Burial Tree which can be either a Ponderosa tree with two distinctive 90 degree bends which point to where the Ute tribal leader is buried or a cedar tree planted to mark the general location of possibly their honored leader's burial site. The location of the tree is relevant to the person who is being honored with this UPT, perhaps indicating his final resting place, where he was born or in the case of a War Chief, where this honored warrior may have fallen in battle.

UPTs with two distinct 90° bends in the trunk, usually found close to the ground, are known as Burial Tree and were said to have been cultivated to honor a tribal leader who had died. This type of Prayer Tree is important in that it commemorates or honors the life and death or passing of a tribal leader from this world to the next. The Ute Indians believed all life comes from the Mother Earth, symbolic of the tree growing up or emerging from the ground. The first 90° bend in the trunk of the Burial Tree, causing the tree trunk to run parallel to the ground, reflects upon how this person walked across the ground in life. The second 90° bend goes upwards in the Prayer Tree tells how the tribal leader has died and ascended towards the Great Spirit.

The Burial Trees observed throughout the Pikes Peak Region were found with various lengths to the portion of the tree trunk running parallel to the ground, varying in length from one to seven or eight feet before ascending upward. There is some speculation that the length of tree trunk after the first bend and before the second one extending skyward, may suggest the lifespan of the person being honored as either a longer or a shorter life. Another unknown is the significance of the direction the tree is pointing, perhaps to where the person was born or died or is buried, but one thing is for certain, the direction the Ute Indian Burial Tree points is not random.

According to the Ute culture if their leaders led a good life the leaders were rewarded after death by joining the Creator, their Father, in the next world. The Ute believed that upon their death, every Ute Indian would be met by a spiritual guide who would lead them before the Creator and serve as an advocate for the good they had accomplished in life. The Ute also believed that fortunately, their spiritual guide was very lenient on specifically what good or bad deeds they had accomplished in life and that most Ute would ultimately be allowed to pass into the next life to be with the Creator.

The Ute Medicine Man or Woman, and other members of the tribe carried cedar seeds. In marking the general location of the burial site, they carefully planted one or possibly two cedar seeds and nurtured them whenever they returned to the site of the tribal leaders' burial location. Ute Elder, Dr. Jefferson believes that the Ute were the only tribe to plant trees for this purpose. If cedar seeds were not available, the use of Ponderosa Pines and other trees would be used for Burial Trees. They would honor the leader and share the story about what the leader had accomplished in life to the younger members of the tribe. The Garden of the Gods, located at the base of Pikes Peak, is the lower entrance to or eastern exit from the Ute Pass and is still lined with Ute Trailmarker Trees. The Garden of the Gods was known to have been used by the Ute for crevice burials, their preferred method of burial. The red rocks of the Garden of the Gods are sprinkled with cedar trees; however, most appear to be too young to have been planted by the Ute Indians.

Trailmarkers in the Garden of the Gods still mark the location of Indian trails leading to the center of the Red Rock formations worn from centuries of use by the Ute and other Native American Indians, including the Plains Indians (Cheyenne and Arapahoe). It was generally accepted that members of different tribes who would meet near the Garden of the Gods were at peace while gathered among the Red Rocks. The Ute used the Ute Pass, a well-known trail which traversed around the north face of Pikes Peak (Tava), which led them from the high mountain meadows and rich hunting grounds, to the Garden of the Gods and from there northeast to the plains east of the Colorado Rocky Mountains.

The grasslands south of the Platte River and north of the Arkansas River were thick with huge herds of bison. Estimates from early explorers, including Zebulon Pike and French trappers, put bison numbers in the millions, perhaps a high as forty million, until the white settlers and buffalo hunters began to arrive in the mid-nineteenth century then bison numbers declined drastically. Tragically, by the end of the nineteenth century the American bison were nearly extinct with perhaps only about one thousand still remaining.

The fact that cedar trees are not indigenous to the Black Forest is one of the strongest indicators the tree was planted and may have been used to mark the location of a Ute burial. Cedar trees are either male or female and cannot populate on their own. This strongly suggests they were deliberately planted at that particular site for a specific purpose. If other UPT varieties are found in the area and if it is along an old trail, the likelihood of it being a Ute Burial Tree is substantially increased. The age of the cedar tree must be fairly old, for they would have been planted at least prior to the 1860's or 1870's when the Ute had access to the land.

I have located only two cedar trees in the Black Forest area and they were found on private property, the first near a well-established old trail that parallels a creek bed and bordered on the west by a Ponderosa Burial Tree with unmistakable ligature marks and a distinctive peeled bark pattern at the first bend of the trunk. Between this Burial Tree and the purposefully planted old Cedar tree, two hiking friends and I located what appeared to be four smaller burial mounds. Although the Ute burials were often in rock crevices or cave entrances, they were also buried in a small pit covered with stones. These would fill in with dirt and over years some would turn into mounds.

These sites were not excavated for various reasons, not the least of which was a lack of specialized archaeological education and training. Federal laws protect Native American sacred sites on government land and any disruption of a Native American sacred or burial site is not to be taken lightly, even on private property. Furthermore, it is a widely held belief within the Native American community that very bad luck will fall upon those who desecrate a grave and worse, that bad luck will also be transferred to the intruder's family.

The second Cedar tree mentioned above was located at the northern base of a rocky outcropping that was at one time volcanic. This location may have also served as an observation point, perhaps even for astrological viewing, and is located within a mile of what appears to have been a sacred gathering place on what is today the La Foret Conference and Events Center. A cursory search of the immediate area did not reveal any burial mounds; however, a more detailed future exploration of the area around the rocky outcropping may prove beneficial.

Story Tree

The forth classification of UPT is the Story or Message Tree. As the name implies, a message tree was likely used to convey a short-term message and directions on how to find certain locations such as a good place to camp or find fresh water. Messages left on Aspen were intended to communicate a short-term message since the lifespan of an Aspen was short. The bark of the Aspen tree can also be easily erased by man or even altered by elk or deer chewing the bark or rubbing their antlers aggressively against the bark.

Petroglyphs, in comparison, last hundreds or even thousands of years dependent upon the hardness of rock used, depth of the carving and/or the exposure to the elements. Message Trees were typically Aspen trees, and have been referred to as Aspen Carvings or Arborglyphs (Arbor as in trees, glyphs as in petroglyphs); however, Ponderosa Pines trees have also been used as Arborglyphs.

An arborglyph, similar to a petroglyph (sometimes called rock art), may have exhibited an artist flare; however, fewer of the older specimens exist due to the shorter lifespan of the Aspen tree. The intent of the message or story being communicated was obviously much shorter in duration since Aspen trees generally only last between eighteen to eighty years; however, a grove of several very large Aspens west of Eleven Mile Canyon in Teller County suggests the lifespan of an Aspen may be somewhat longer.

The few confirmed Aspen Ute Indian Message or Story Trees that remain in existence today are usually found in museums; however most, if not all, types of Ute Culturally Modified Trees tell a story. It would be difficult to confirm Aspen carvings found on a living tree in a forest today without some other definitive evidence as the tree would probably not be old enough to have been carved by anyone from the Ute Native American Indian Tribes. To further complicate the authentication processes, other inhabitants of the mountains in Colorado, particularly southern Colorado, were heavily grazed by sheep, and the Mexican sheepherders were known to also mark trees especially Aspen trees, to denote a message such as a geographical boundary.

The lifespan of a Ponderosa, in contrast, is 800 years, and several of the Bristlecone Pine trees found at higher altitudes are thought to be 2000 years old. Story Trees made in these trees would last for a longer period of time and help the Elders tell the Ute's oral history, which were often recounted in story form. Events such as a successful hunt or perhaps the outcome of a major battle would be retold for generations as stories. The bark of the Ponderosa Pine appears to have been used as a preferred medium in which to carve figures. It is also believed that many UPTs were intended for ceremonies, such as the Sun Dance, which seems especially true with the last variety described next, the Prophecy Tree.

Prophecy Tree

The Prophecy Tree sometimes referred to as a Providence Tree or Intertwined Tree is the fifth and final type or variety of Ute Indian Prayer Tree (UPT). It is perhaps the most interesting and possibly the rarest and hardest to find. Where other UPTs, especially the Message or Story Tree, tells of a past event, the Prophecy Tree is believed to be the only UPT and possibly the only CMT believed to foretell of a future event, of someone or something of major significance yet to come. Ute Indian Prophecy Trees are more complex in design and obviously much harder to cultivate. These UPT would have required more energy, greater vision, and time to cultivate, perhaps even generations.

Prophecy or Intertwined Trees are sometimes found growing together where the trunks have become fused and would have required significant cultivation of a single tree or perhaps two or more separate trees. While still very young, just saplings, Prophecy Trees would require periodic grooming or cultivation, over a period of several years, perhaps even several generations of Ute Tribal Members.

These fascinating trees may have started as two separate trees that were transplanted or somehow positioned to grow together. Other Prophecy Trees may have been one tree separated at its base to appear as if it is two separate trees. The branches of these trees are often shaped or possibly even removed and other limbs may possibly have been grafted from the same tree or extracted from a different tree. The branch may have been connected to the trunk indicating a specific directionality or even interconnected to another branch. On a few occasions trees had the bark split to allow two or more trees to grow together, become fused as one single unit or formation.

One example of a Prophecy Tree found in the Fox Run Regional Park that we call the Hugging Tree, has one tree that appears to be a younger tree with its branches wrapped around an older taller tree. At about 20 feet above the ground level it appears as if the branches of the younger tree reach around to embrace or hug the other slightly larger tree. Another Prophecy Tree that has been named the Portal Tree is one that is very intricately shaped with clear evidence of a portion of the lower bark being peeled away. The location of this tree is also intriguing for it is found on a straight trajectory from what is believed to be the oldest UPT in the park and possibly the oldest in Black Forest, referred to as Grandmother. The Portal Tree points towards Tava (Pikes Peak).

These three trees, the Grandmother, The Portal and the Hugging Tree can easily be placed in Story Tree and Portal Tree Categories, all tell a story that is interrelated. During our hike with the Ute it was pointed out that the Grandmother Story Tree points to the Portal tree that when passing through takes you up hill to view Tava, all in a straight line.

Alternative Categories for UPTs and Other Trees Sacred to the Ute

Each of the five main types of UPTs listed above used to help categorize UPT can have peeled bark, but not all do. Also, not all trees that have peeled bark have had it peeled for medicinal purposes. Types of CMT can overlap. Should all trees that exhibit bark that has been peeled be considered a Ute Medicine Tree? Is there another distinct variety of UPT that has peeled bark for utility purposes only, such as food that should be in a separate category? Because the original purpose of the peeling may never be known I have categorized them all Ute Medicine Trees, but others have named them differently. It is important to remember that we classify these amazing trees as a way for us to understand them.

Also, there are various other trees that have been modified or used by the Ute. These trees are rare and worth mentioning.

Peeled Bark Tree, American Indian Utility Trees

In a short yet informative 24 page treatise by Jack R. Williams which he entitled, *American Indian Culture Trees, Living History*, Mr. Williams describes two important varieties of CMTs which he attributes to the Ute Indians. Mr. Williams describes what he referred to as American Indian Utility Trees and Ute Ceremonial Trees and provides several excellent photographs along with a written description of each variety of trees he has found in the Florissant area west of Pikes Peak. American Indian Utility Trees were described by Mr. Williams as, "Ponderosa pines were scarred (harvested) when they were young-20 to 40 years of age."

Mr. Williams continues to write, "During this stage the bark is gray-brown to black being relatively smooth and thin which allows easier cutting and peeling. As the tree grows and ages its bark structure changes to a reddish orange color of broad irregular scaly plates creating a natural armor. The mature trees are quite tough to peel so were probably not sought for food. Pitch, of course, could continue to be gathered for the life of the tree. The Indian Culture trees we see today were scarred well over 130 years ago (in 2001)…fall harvested cambium were undoubtedly made as this was the time when the Ute mashed and cooked it to form sweet cakes for winter use."

In this publication, Mr. Williams writes of a discussion he held with a Ute, Curtis Fair, who explained, "…my uncle told me that Bristlecone pine sap was heated and mixed with beeswax (to keep it from crystallizing) and used as a glue to help fasten points to arrows." To his credit, Mr. Williams conducted what he referred to as a, "Bristlecone Pitch-Beeswax Glue Experiment" fastening a metal trade arrowhead inserted in the end of an arrow shaft (with two-parts sap and one-part beeswax) and found that a sinew wrap point is solidly anchored. Mr. Williams relates that it is a mistake to believe that all American Indian Culture Trees have a spiritual connection, such as the Ute Ceremonial Tree, for many were used as American Indian Utility Trees.

Mr. Williams went on to write, "Aside from the cambium's use as food and medicine, the resin, with the turpentine evaporated out, was collected in globs and chewed like gum to clean the teeth and ground up to be used in medicines such as laxative tea. The Florissant area is not unique to these great scarred Ponderosa pines. They are found throughout the state and elsewhere in some numbers throughout the 'original Ute domain' to include the Rio Grande, San Juan, Uncompahgre, Gunnison, Pike and San Isabel National Forests, Mesa Verde National Park, and the Great Sand Dunes National Park and Preserve, as well as Bureau of Land Management and private lands…"

Mr. Williams goes on to explain, "The blazing of pine trees is an extremely widespread trait among American Indians in their utilization of them. This writer has observed scars cut similarly from the Flathead Reservation in Montana south to the southern tip of the Guadalupe Mountains in Texas, and west to the Lukachukas (Chuska) Mountains and Navajo Mountain areas of the Navajo Reservation, plus much of western Colorado; and also in northern California where the great basket making tribes lived."

Depicting photographs of a blazed Ponderosa pine tree near Florissant, Colorado, estimated to be over 180 years old, with a close-up of the base of the same tree taken in 1999 shows an accumulation of pine resin at the bottom of the cut scar, Mr. Williams further describes, "Pines were and are used for food, shelter, fuel, medicine, deodorant, chewing gum, waterproofing, beds, cradleboards, smoking hides, tools, paints, and in basketry – roots and the long needles. In some cases, pines are venerated as being sacred."

Under the heading "How Pines Were Used" as a food source, Mr. Williams describes, "Cambium was eaten by almost all American Indians living in and near pine forests…The Ute Cochetopa Agency annual report for 1870 said the people peeled bark from many trees for food or medicine (Simons, p. 135). Again, the Agency reported that during the winter of 1876-1877, when the government rations were almost nonexistent and the Ute were starving near Cimarron, they peeled bark from trees (Simmons, p. 170). This type of situation could explain a large number of scarred trees in a relatively small area. In the 1890s, Ute along the Dolores River were seen grinding cambium and mixing it with corn, making what they called "pitch corn" (Martorano)."

As a medicine, Mr. Williams wrote, "The Ponderosa pine of the High Rockies was a chosen source of resin for ointments and plasters. The inner bark of the white pine was preferred for poultices, which were applied to burns and sores. It was claimed new skin would come quickly and without a scar…Pine resin was one of the most important sources of remedies of the Indians of New Mexico, where it was called the "cure-all." Pinon pine was considered a medicinal godsend to people living in the shadows of the Sangre de Cristos and other ranges of the Rockies. Boiled tea of needles was drunk for diarrhea, nausea, and fever…Its resin was mixed with native tobacco and salt, spread on a cloth, and laid on the temples to relieve a headache."

Under his section for "Kanosh", Basket Water Jars, Mr. Williams describes how the early Pueblo people (Basketmakers), and later the Paiutes, "trait of using pine resin dates back to before 600 B.C. in the Southwest"…to waterproof their water jar baskets. He describes how resin, primarily from Pinon pine, was used by the, "Ute (who) were more skilled in making baskets which they constructed from willow and sumac (Rhus trilobata). The most characteristic of these was the water jug, which was an urn-shaped basket covered with a waterproofing coating of pitch" (Rockwell)…adding, "Some Ute women pitch-coated only the inside of their water baskets, similar to their neighbors, the Jicarilla Apaches. Their baskets were often coated on the outside with a white clay, and some had leather fastened to the bottom to lessen the wear."

"Water baskets were made during the winter when women were sitting around talking. For waterproofing the baskets a certain kind of sap was boiled until it was very sticky. Small round pebbles from the riverbed were added when the sap was poured into the basket, and the basket was rolled around and shaken so the pebbles would work the sap into the grooves of the basket" (Pettit). "…the Ute lifestyle required a great number of "kanosh," as they called them", and could hold between three quarts to 2 and a half gallons of water."

According to a more recent report (1989) written by arborist Marylyn Martorano, forty culturally peeled trees were cored from three different areas of Colorado and the majority were determined to have been peeled between 1815 and 1875. In the writing of Celinda Kaelin, she cites an official letter to the Secretary of War written in 1873 by Lieutenant E.H. Ruffner U.S. Army who had been sent on a reconnaissance of Ute country in Colorado. In his letter Lt. Ruffner stated that the Ute trail to Cochetopa Pass was, "well worn, and the peeled trees show that the valley has been much frequented by Indians." This 140 year old report from Lt. Ruffner is one of the earliest documented references found on peeled trees in the Pikes Peak Region.

Council Tree

As the name implies, a Council Tree was used by Native Americans to indicate a location of a meeting or council, usually a war or peace council with other Native American Tribes or later in the mid-nineteenth Century, with non-Native people to negotiate a treaty or an agreement. As the U.S. evolved, throughout the Nineteenth Century, it was determined that a treaty could only be ratified with another country; therefore, all subsequent agreements the U.S. would enter into with Native Americans would be called an agreement (e.g., The 1880 Ute Agreement).

There is what is known as the Ute Council Tree located at the confluence of the Uncompahgre and Gunnison Rivers in the Southwest part of Colorado, near the town of Delta. This majestic old 85 foot tall cottonwood tree dates back to 1802; however, it appears that it may have served more as a location mark, where the Ute would gather in council as opposed to having been modified to provide direction. This tree is an important and historic old Ute tree that was later dedicated to Chief Ouray and his wife, Chipeta, who may have been the only woman ever permitted to sit in council.

Ute Ceremonial Trees

Another type of tree important to the Ute was the Ute Ceremonial Tree. On the Three Eagles Ranch located just north of the El Paso County line, I walked with ranch owners, Paula and Rollie Johnson and discovered a majestic old Ute Ceremonial Tree displaying an identical ceremonial scar at the base of the tree, as shown in photographs of Ute Ceremonial Trees found in the Florissant area and described by Jack Williams and Midge Harbour in her book *The Tarryall Mountains and the Puma Hills, A History*, published in 1982.

Midge married Frank Harbour in 1977 and they lived on his Harbour Valley Ranch in Tarryall for 13 years before she moved to Colorado Springs for health reasons. Mrs. Harbour described in her book how the, "Indians made many trips through Tarryall valley into the area where Lake George and Florissant now stand and then went up to Divide and down Ute Pass to Manitou Springs which they called 'Bubbling Waters'. They believed the springs had great medicinal qualities. Many of the eastern plains Indians also visited the springs and gradually worked their way over the passes to the hunting grounds of South Park. The Ute found it necessary to post sentries on strategic points to watch for these enemies. Many battles between the different tribes took place in South Park."

"The Ute performed a dignified and awesome ceremony call the Sun Dance. It demanded much endurance from the participants. For four days and four nights, without food or drink, the dancers stayed in a circular enclosure open to the east and danced facing a central pole, usually a large tree. Each dancer wore a special cape or blanket and blew on a bone whistle. The dancers moved directly toward the pole forward and backward to music made by drummers and singers…Such a tree is still standing across from the Tarryall Road about half way between Lake George and Jefferson."

In her book Midget Harbour also identifies what she calls a Ute Ceremonial Tree located a few miles northwest of Lake George, Colorado. The massive Ponderosa pine is pictured in her book. This Ute Ceremonial Tree, was estimated to be at least 300 years old and is located on the old Vic and Edith Williams homestead north of Tarryall Creek. Edith Williams shared that when she was a young bride, she witnessed many visits by the Ute to this tree, marked with a large peeled bark pattern facing to the southwest, performing ceremonies around the tree in the springtime that included dance and music.

She described how, "Still visible a century later, is a depressed area around the tree in a semi-circle worn into the dirt by the moccasins worn on the feet of the Ute who danced around this Ceremonial Tree." When the Ute left, Edith claimed they often left behind some items at the base of the tree or tied to the branches, often small strips of cloth. Judging by the season, springtime, the ceremony the Ute may have been celebrating could have been the Bear Dance, a dance where the female dancer chooses her male dance partner.

The couples dance back and forth to the rhythm of moraches, notched wooden sticks or rasps, sometimes referred to as bear growlers, which are rubbed rapidly with another stick or sometimes an elk antler while one end rested on hollow log. This dance, sometimes called the Woman's Step Dance is intended to explore the couple's compatibility as well as the other partner's endurance and often leads to marriage. The Tarryall area, as well as much of the mountain region around today's Lake George, remains abundant with wildlife, including the bear that is awakening from their winter's hibernation early in the springtime. The Bear Dance, along with the Sun Dance, is still recognized today by the Ute as important ceremonies to continue their rich culture.

Vortex or Spiral Tree

There exists the possibility of yet another variety of UTP, the Vortex Tree. This UPT variety is much harder to understand and harder to explain, but it is believed to have been cultivated or grown in or near a vortex that contributed to the spiral shape of the tree. A vortex may be affected by the earth's electromagnetic field (EMF or EM field) and to most Native Americans, and almost certainly to the Ute, a vortex may mark a sacred place believed to have a significant spiritual connection to this particular place on Mother Earth. Some people suggest a vortex may also serve as a portal or gateway to another place, to space or perhaps to another dimension.

I have spoken with two women of Native American descent who shared their experiences when "spinning" or turning around in a circle, and feeling a sensation which one woman described as a tingling up her forearms. She described how in certain areas on her property, known to have been frequented by the Ute, if she turned in a counter-clockwise direction, she would experience a masculine sensation, and as she would spin in a clockwise direction, in other locations on her property, she felt what she described as a feminine spiritual connection to the land, to Mother Earth, through this vortex.

The geographical area where this phenomenon was said to be felt has been visited on several occasions by me, and although no sensation was ever personally experienced, this area was rich with UPTs and geological rock formations, including water retention basins and troughs which can be confidently attributed to the Ute of a long past era. Interestingly enough, this same area also has a high incident rate of reported UFO activity, with more than one report coming from credible sources.

Although several spiral shaped UPT have been discovered throughout the Pikes Peak Region, most, if not all, have been found to be spiraling in a clockwise direction as they extend upward. It appears that most Vortex or Spiral Trees, sometimes referred to as Dwarf Trees, are somewhat smaller in size, which may have been caused by manipulation or modification, with evidence of tie-down or ligature marks, observable on most Spiral Trees and the majority can be found with the distinctive Ute Peeled Bark pattern. However, without a primary or even secondary source data, it is very difficult to list a Vortex Tree as a separate and distinct UPT variety. It remains somewhat of an enigma if Vortex Trees actual exist. Spiral shaped Ute Prayer Trees do remain intriguing specimens to study and perhaps future knowledge will advance their understanding.

Cat Face Tree

Perhaps one of the most fascinating, scarce and lesser known of the different subgroups of UPTs is the Cat Face. Several of my tree hunting friends and I have found 6-8 unusually scarred Ponderosa Trees in the Black Forest that appeared to have been scarred with fire 4-6 feet off the ground. Lightning strikes and forest fires were not believed to be the cause. These Cat Faces do appear to be an artifact from some form of human interaction years ago.

On a research trip to the Southern Ute Reservation with two friends, Vern Kuykendall and Phil Tinsley, we were told of the existence of a 4-inch (thick) file containing some information about CMTs, including the documentation of a failed attempt to transplant a few Ute Prayer Trees to the Southern Ute Culture Center and Museum (SUCCM) in Ignacio, Colorado. It took several months, but finally with the assistance of the then Acting-Executive Director, Nathan Strong Elk, this file was recovered from the SUCCM archive, converted into a PDF, and studies revealed several primary source interviews with Ute Tribal Elders, including Berta Cuch and Clifford Duncan (Northern Ute Reservation). Buried in this archive file was a reference under Pine Trees describing how Cat Faces were caused by resting burning wood against the tree for an extended period of time, causing the fire to burn away portions of the tree revealing an image that often resembled what the Ute thought looked like the face of a cat or cougar. These scarred burned areas were described as being rectangle or triangular, in shape, started 1-2 feet above the ground, extended upward for 4-6 feet, and were usually found on the uphill side of the slope burned into a Ponderosa Pine tree.

Commonly referred to as a mountain lion, the cougar or puma who hunts across much of the mountainous regions of South and North American, was well known to the Ute and respected as a fierce predator for much of the same big game animals that were hunted by the Ute (i.e., deer, elk, moose, bison, antelope). Interestingly, there are more names for the cougar or puma than any other animal (Guinness World's Record lists forty different names to be precise), including the mountain screamer, mountain cat and catamount, which is likely a derivative from cat of the mountain.

However, the reference to the cougar by its most common name, a mountain lion, is technically incorrect since the cougar does not roar like a lion and does not have a mane. The Ute no doubt knew the puma for centuries; however, the first reference to the cougar as a mountain lion was not recorded until the first year of the Pikes Peak Gold Strike in a reference in 1858 of this huge cat by George A. Jackson of Colorado.

Another grouping or cluster of Cat Faces have been found in Custer County, southeast of Pikes Peak on the northeastern slope of a hill located on the Bear Basin Ranch owned by Gary Ziegler and Amy Finger. It was believed by the Ute that each tree had a spirit and that if the Creator chose; he would reveal the spirit of the tree after fire was placed against the trunk. It appears the thick bark of the selected Ponderosa tree was split or partially peeled away before the burning wood was taken from the fire and placed against the tree.

Although some of the images may require the use of one's imagination, images such as a cougar or an elk have been discovered. And on one occasion, and appropriately so, the image of a bear was discovered on the Bear Basin Ranch, near Westcliffe, Colorado. In another location on the La Foret property in El Paso County, the use of a smartphone facial recognition was deployed and the image revealed appears to be that of a helmeted Spanish Conquistador.

Bow Bank Tree

One final lesser known type or possible sub-classification of a UPT is the Bow Bank, which is actually a block of wood that had been carefully extracted from a Juniper Tree and used by the Ute to fashion a bow. What remains visible running vertically up the tree of the Juniper is a void in the trunk, approximately 10-12 inches in width and 20-24 inches in height, where the block of wood was extracted. It is believed that prayer was associated with the extraction of the block of wood or bank, from which the bow would be craved. While harvesting the wood and fashioning the bow and arrows, it is believed the Ute offered prayer to the Creator to help guide them in the effective use of the bow. The bow and arrows were important to the Ute for defense and for hunting to sustain their families and as the living tree had a spirit, it was important to ask for guidance from that spirit for the arrows to fly straight and strong and true.

Arrows, sometimes called darts, shot from wooden bows were used as a means of defense of the Ute warrior's tribe or used for hunting game for food to sustain one's tribe. The bow string could be made from several substances, but the tendons of a large game animal such as an elk were preferable.

Bow Banks are extremely rare; in fact, I have spotted only one possible tree candidate on a nearly inaccessible cliff face in Fremont County, so my limited information comes from a handful of photographs of these rare trees, but they have been confirmed to exist by a Ute Elder. It is believed that great care was given so as to not take too large of a block or bank of wood from the trunk of the Juniper, so as to not jeopardize the life of the tree.

Ute Tribal Elder, Dr. Jefferson, also confirmed the existence of the Bow Bank tree and told me there were also Medicine Wheel Trees, which resemble the configuration of the Ute Medicine Wheel, anchored by four primary trees aligned to the four cardinal directions (north, east, south, and west) and point towards one another in a circular configuration. The Medicine Wheel Trees were mentioned during a hike in the Black Forest of northern El Paso County, when Dr. Jefferson pointed out a distinctive circular pattern between a cluster of UPTs; however, the west and north trees could not be located, and it remains a mystery if these other two trees were cut down or ever existed in the first place.

Another grouping of three large Ponderosa Pines found in Black Forest just off Baptist Road, definitively display a correlation between them, with one to the north, one to the east and a third to the south. These three trees appear to be of approximately the same age and were likely modified at approximately the same time. There is another Trailmarker Tree just off the north side of the pavement which points to this cluster of three trees. When speculating why there was not a tree to the west, I recalled earlier instructional lessons provided by Dr. Jefferson who said the Ute always approached their Sacred Trees from the west.

Identifying UPTS

Identifying UPTs can be difficult. Prior to placing UPTs into a category first it must be determined if it really is a UPT and not naturally deformed. When studying a possible UPT candidate it is helpful to compare the characteristics against a known or confirmed UPT of a similar variety. When trying to identify if a tree is a UPT, look for ligature marks, peeled bark, other modified trees in the area, direction the tree is pointing, if there is water nearby, creek, or significant location that it might be pointing. Also in identifying if a tree may be a UPT, it is worth referring to a short yet informative 24 page treatise by Jack R. Williams which he entitled, *American Indian Culture Trees, Living History*, in which Williams writes "How Pine Trees Can Become Deformed." Ways that pine trees can be deformed would include:

- Nature: Weather, wind, snow, cold, lightning, fire, disease, mistletoe, drought, flood

- Man interference: Breaking, twisting, cutting, logging, vehicles

- Animal interference: grazing,

- Location: rocks in the way of growth

Determining the age of a tree and if it is old enough to have been modified by the Ute when they were actively modifying trees is another way to determine if a tree could be a UPT. Dendrochronology, the science of counting tree rings to determine the age of a tree, is perhaps the best way to determine the date the tree began to grow, and in some cases may actually indicate when the cultural modification might have occurred. Determining the precise age of a living tree can prove challenging; even coring a UPT to count the rings can be misleading due to the misshaping of the tree trunk caused by the modification or distortion or twisting of the trunk. Furthermore, the Ute strongly discourage coring a tree to determine its age as they believe it is harmful to the tree. It is important to remember the Ute is an ancient culture who respects trees as living entities, each with a spirit of their own.

This belief is shared by other indigenous tribal peoples and is sometimes referred to as animism. Animism is not a word that exists in the Native American language, possibly because it is simply accepted as a foundational or world view belief that all human and non-human entities possess a spiritual essence including animals, rocks, plants and trees. The term animism became somewhat popularized by the work of anthropologist Sir Edward Taylor, in his book *Primitive Culture* published in 1871. Taylor makes reference to the animism belief as being typical of "cognitive underdevelopment" common with primitive people "living in hunter gatherer societies." Many of Taylor's contemporaries expressed their options that there was no distinction between the intellectual capabilities of what Taylor referred to as "savages" and westerners who were well-educated and distinguishable he felt by a certain level of sophistication. A study of the Ute tree modification practices and traditions clearly demonstrates the Ute were a far more advanced culture than simply people living in a hunter gatherer society.

Many suspected Culturally Modified Trees that are believed to have been modified by the Ute that have been observed in the Pikes Peak Region are very small in circumference and shorter in height. While counting the tree rings of dead trees can be a very accurate indicator of the age of a tree, determining the age of a living tree based simply on size can be quite difficult to ascertain with any degree of accuracy. Although the shape, height and circumference of a living tree can be a good indication of its age, several smaller UPTs in the Black Forest appear as if their growth has been stunted almost giving the appearance of a dwarf tree, with twisted limbs and spiraling trunks that somewhat resemble larger versions of the Japanese Bonsai Trees.

Interviews with many residents in the Black Forest area, including several of whom have lived on the same property between 10 to 25 years, a few even longer, give varying reports on tree growth. Some accounts indicate a Ponderosa tree may easily grow 10 to 20 feet in height over a ten years' period of time, where other eyewitness accounts can point to other Ponderosa trees located in the same forest that have not grown more than 3 to 4 inches in height in over a quarter of a century, if at all.

It is well understood that the tree's type, geographical terrain, soil composition, altitude, access to water or even the competition for sunlight can cause the height and girth (diameter) to vary within even short distances of one another. If, for example, the tree must compete with other trees nearby for sunlight, it might need to grow taller in order to thrive. Absent competition for sunlight from other trees may cause the same tree to grow fuller, again dependent upon soil and other factors such as altitude. At an elevation of 7,704 feet above sea level, the Black Forest has the highest elevation east of the Rocky Mountains to the Atlantic Ocean. The next highest point all the way to the east coast is Mount Washington in the White Mountains of New Hampshire which is the tallest peak in the northeastern United States with an elevation of 6,288 feet above sea level.

Mr. Williams also provides a partial list of counties (Park, Teller) where American Indian Culture Trees can be found, including the Indian Grove area, located within the Great Sand Dunes National Park in Saguache County, Colorado. He describes a, "concentration of seventy-two mature Ponderosa pines, many marked by large scars. Archaeologists believe that the scarring occurred when Ute Indians peeled the bark from these trees, and that the site can provide important information…the majority of these culturally modified trees were peeled between 1816 and 1848." These are old trees and worth protecting because once they're gone, they won't be coming back.

The history of the Ute, as with most Native Americans, is predominately oral dependent. Their culture is evaporating with the passing of each successive generation, including their sacred CMT practices. This occurrence may be further complicated by their deeply held belief that the most sacred of Ute secrets can only be revealed to another Ute or to a non-Native, only after an individual outside the tribe has proven himself or herself worthy of being trusted with such sensitive knowledge. Most of us non-Natives may therefore be prohibited from having any better understanding of the UPT varieties or purposes, especially for the sacred ceremonial trees. A better understanding of exactly how many types or classifications of Ute Prayer Trees actually exist or ever existed may forever remain shrouded in mystery.

Fox Run Ute Trailmarker: This impressive Ute Trailmarker Tree is one of an important pair of Trailmarker Trees located in Fox Run Regional Park, El Paso, Colorado. This classic Ute Trailmarker Tree displays the distinctive 30° upward bend, telltale withered primary trunk (extending in the photo to the upper left or 10 o'clock position) and a faint ligature mark around the inside of the curve evidence of where the tree was staked down. This photo was taken while standing on the foot trail northwest of a narrow wooden foot bridge facing south. Directly across the dry creek to the east is an identical Ute Trailmarker tree pointing in the exact same direction, southeast. It is not known what exactly this location meant two hundred plus years ago when the two trees were modified; however, there are several significant locations in that direction including a major natural spring and tributary source for the Black Squirrel Creek which feeds into Monument Creek, then Fountain Creek and the Arkansas River. If one were to reverse that direction, starting from the Mississippi River, then tracing the Arkansas River, Fountain Creek, while staying on the left bank and within walking distance of these important sources of water, you would arrive at this exact location, especially if you were to follow the Trailmarker Trees or occasional rock cairns (which were always at risk of being moved for reuse). This Trailmarker Tree and its mate 75 yards south across the creek, are best studied as a pair. The second Trailmarker Tree carries the traditional peeled bark pattern of the Ute Medicine Man, while this Trailmarker Tree closer to the foot trail displays a much small (6-8 inch) notched area on the west side of the trunk about three feet above the ground. This chop mark is most likely not from a Ute as it was done without consideration for collecting the calcium rich cambium layer. This chop mark is consistent with the white man, known as a trailblazer, who wanted to mark or blaze a trail and would mark the tree with upper and downward chops with an ax. This Trailmarker Tree is also a perfect example of how the tree modifies its cellular structure to support the massive weight by taking on an oval shape to the trunk below the bend.

Black Forest Burial Tree: This intriguing Ute Burial Tree is located in the Black Forest, on private ranch property east of the Pineries Open Space, El Paso County, Colorado. This tree was partially burned during the 2013 Black Forest Fire, but did survive the fire which ravaged the surrounding trees and houses and claimed the lives of two Black Forest residents. The tough bark of a Ponderosa Pine tree can grow to be an inch and a half thick and will help protect the tree from fire. Unless a fire reaches the top or crown of a Ponderosa many times they will survive. An inspection of the land six months after this deadly wildland fire revealed several stone artifacts which had been previously covered by pine needles and dead grass, including a circular stone firepit and what appeared to be nearby burial mound. Ute Burial Trees were modified to honor the life of a Ute Tribal member and each tree was deliberately selected, intentionally directed and skillfully cultivated while the tree was still very young and pliable. Burial Trees would have had some reference to the person being honored, such as a Ute warrior who may have fallen in battle defending their tribe, which was among the highest honors a Ute male could achieve. The Ute were required to return four times to pray at each tree which would have allowed them at least four seasons to return to modify a tree. The direction this Burial Tree points is towards the high plains northeast of the Black Forest where buffalo were hunted. Some trees were used to drape hides over so hair could be scraped off then dried. The shape and size of this CMT somewhat resembles an American Bison, although its true purpose will forever remain a mystery. This Burial Tree is very similar to the one found along the hike in Fox Run Regional Park.

Fox Run Medicine Tree: Pictured here in the foreground is a fascinating Ute Medicine Tree and in the background a second similar shaped Ute Prayer Tree is also visible. Not visible from this view are two ancient Ute Trailmarker Trees and two Ute Burial Trees located within 50-75 yards of one another, which adds to the possibility this site may have been a sacred destination location. Both trees display evidence of multiple human interventions that would have required multiple seasonal visits over a period of many years, possibly extending over several generations. In addition to its twisted trunk and peeled bark on the back of the trunk, a scorched burnt area can be seen on inside the peeled bark which may have been ceremonial in nature. The huge bulbous outgrowth, about five feet above ground level, and several ligature marks are clearly visible on the inside of the upper twisted curve shown at the top left of the photo. The estimated age of one of the nearby Trailmarker Trees, based upon the full orange color of the trunk, as opposed to core samples, is thought to be between 450-550 years old. The oldest UPT could predate not only the founding of the United States of America, but perhaps even the discovery of the Americas by Columbus (1492). When speaking of the discovery of America with Ute Elder Dr. Jefferson, he quickly pointed out they (Native Americans) were pretty sure they knew where it was all along. These two trees are located in Fox Run Regional Park, El Paso County, Colorado.

Trailmarker Trees pointing to a Burial Tree: This trio of trees found in Fox Run Regional Park is a prime example of the importance of the Black Forest area to the Ute shown by the numerous UPTs in the local area. If you follow the direction the tree in the forefront of this photo is pointing and look across the distance and a little to the northwest, you can see another Trailmarker Tree pointing in the direction to this tree, except a little to the southwest. Between the two trees is a large Burial Tree. All three of these trees are very old and modified approximately during the same time as all three trees are similar in size and color. The Burial tree is hard to spot in the picture as it is in the shadow, but during the UPT hike of this area the Trailmarker Trees can be clearly seen marking the location of the Burial Tree. This Trailmarker Tree, photographed from a different angle, is displayed on the back cover of this book.

Story Tree: This tree has been referred to as the Grandmother Tree by those who have hiked the park and are interested in Ute Prayer Trees. It has been called Grandmother due to its age and its outstretched arms like a Grandmother welcomes her grandchildren. It is an example of the forth classification of UPT, the Story or Message Tree. The respectful name reflects the age of the tree. We do not know the original message this tree had to tell, but it is in a direct line from the lower section of this area leading to the top of the ridge and the Prophecy Tree that frames Pikes Peak. Like many UPTs this tree has many markings to show that it was modified over many years.

Prophecy Tree - Ute Portal Tree: This fascinating Ute Prayer Tree is located in the Fox Run Regional Park, in northern El Paso County, Colorado. It is believed these are actually two separate trees that have been sculpted into what we see today. The tree on the left separates unnaturally at the top to form what resembles a football goalpost with the right extending arm connecting to the second tree which points unmistakably toward Tava (Pikes Peak). These are older Ponderosa Pine trees, as evident by the color of their nearly full orange bark, and the tree on the right in the photo displays the classic peeled bark pattern of the Ute Medicine Man near the base (not visible from this photo angle). This peeled bark pattern is wider than most and may have been removed during a ceremony and possibly used for constructing a cradleboard. Cradleboards were expertly crafted by the Ute women who traditionally carried Ute children strapped in a cradleboard carried on their back from one camp to the next until the child was old enough to walk on their own (at about age three). The Cherokee use a similar goalpost type design as a boundary marker; however, theirs extend outward from the ground where these two trunks separate about 7-8 feet above ground level. These two trees give the impression they could have been used symbolically or ceremonially with an opening that represents a portal, which gives it the name the Portal Tree. Downhill a few hundred yards from this tree is what is known as the Grandmother Tree which is believed to be the oldest tree in the Park.

Prophecy Tree: The fifth and last generally accepted type or variety of Ute Prayer Tree is the Prophecy Tree, sometimes referred to as an Intertwined Tree. These are possibly the rarest CMTs found in Colorado and are the only type of Ute Prayer Trees that are said to foretell of someone or something to come; like a prophet or prophecy. Where the other four Ute Prayer Tree types or varieties tell of something in the past, such as where a battle had been fought or where water had been found in the past, the Prophecy Tree tells of something yet to occur. This Prophecy Tree is several hundred years old and was skillfully modified, appearing almost to have been sculpted. The limbs resemble outstretched arms that appear to reach around the other slightly larger tree in a loving embrace. The thick bark of the taller Ponderosa tree has been split by lightening from above where they touch to the ground allowing the two trees to grow together; perhaps symbolizing two becoming one. This meadow is a very tranquil peaceful setting and reminds one of a cathedral, with the surround tall Ponderosas serving as church spires. Standing to the right of the tree is Vern Kuykendall, wearing the hat, and to the left is Phil Tinsley, my two friends who have been instrumental in conducting the field research and helping to reconnect the Ute of today with the sacred trees modified years ago by their tribal ancestors. This rare Prophecy Tree is located in Fox Run Regional Park, El Paso County, Colorado.

Trailmarker: This fascinating old Ute Trailmarker Tree is located on a trail in the Fox Run Regional Park of northern El Paso County, Colorado. The tree displays clear evidence of human interaction in the distant past and the distance above the ground, when considered with its location along the east side of a well-worn trail, suggests it may have been modified by a Ute while on horseback. This practice of marking a tree at a height visible while on horseback was known to have been in practice by the Ute in marking trails. The Ute preferred to travel along a ridge line so game or approaching enemy could be observed from either side of the ridge. This Ute Prayer Tree displays multiple ligature marks as well as a peeled bark pattern which extends down the trunk. At the first major bend to the trunk, approximately 8 feet above the ground, the trunk was noticeably constricted then redirected to point towards the south. There are several other intriguing Ute Prayer Trees in the immediate vicinity including one on the west side of the trail with a set of spiral cut scars descending down the trunk with what appears to have been for the purpose of collecting pine pitch. Several trees in the park have been stuck by lightning, which can leave a twisted deformation of the trunk; however this tree bears definite indications of being modified by human hands long ago. From this ridge line Tava (Pikes Peak) comes into full view to the west and the high plains are easily accessible to the north as one crosses over the Arkansas/Platte Divide (today's Palmer Divide).

Chapter 4 – Tour of Ute Indian Prayer Trees
in the Pikes Peak Region
Respect the Elders for they know the way; Elders and children always eat first.

I
f you go in search of the historically rich Culturally Modified Trees (CMT) in El Paso County, Colorado, you would be hard pressed to find a better place to start your quest than in the Fox Run Regional Park. Although the Black Forest was frequented by many Native American Indian Tribes including the Cheyenne, Arapahoe, Sioux, Comanche, Ute and Cherokee, only the Cheyenne, Ute and Cherokee were known to have modified trees as part of their cultures. Of those three, only the Ute had a sustained access throughout all of the Shining Mountains for years that would have been required to culturally modify these sacred trees.

It is a mistake to identify every bent or disfigured tree in the Black Forest or elsewhere, as a CMT, just as it would be a mistake to attribute every CMT to the Ute Nation. There is a primary source regarding peeled bark trees in the notes of John Wesley Powell. During the winter of 1868-1869, Powell and his survey team stayed on the White River Reservation. His firsthand account described the Ute tradition of peeling the bark of the Ponderosa to extract the mucilaginous substance located between the outer bark and the inner hardwood which was used for medicinal and nutritional purposes.

When trying to positively identify a UPT in the Pikes Peak Region, it is also important to recognize what other contributing factors can naturally cause the trunk of a tree to become bent or its limbs to become twisted or disfigured. Lightning strikes are prevalent throughout the summer months and the tall Ponderosa Pines are a favorite target, often blowing out sections of bark and leaving a tell-tale signature of a downward spiral pattern. Mistletoe is also pervasive in certain areas of the forest and leaves behind the distinctive blacken twisted branches reminiscent of the "witches' broom."

Heavy snowfall can cause a younger tree to bend over succumbing to the weight, and barbed wire can leave what appears to be a tie down or ligature mark if a tree happened to have been used as a fence post at one time or another. Insects or, more often than not, birds in pursuit of the nutritious beetle can leave a tree disfigured. Deer or elk can leave damaged bark from where they chewed the bark or rubbed the felt from their antlers in the spring. Porcupines love to nest up high in the pine tree, munching on the tender branches nearby. Only by studying what other natural occurring factors can cause a tree to become bent or disfigured, can one eventually gain confidence in ruling out natural causes and decide if a tree was modified through human intervention.

It is also important not to judge a single tree by itself; rather it is vital to take in the surrounding geographical environment in search of a collective body of evidence to support a conclusion. Is this tree part of a larger ecosystem, consisting of creeks, old trails and found in a cluster of other likely UPTs? This clustering effect also helps one to conclude this is not a natural phenomenon because this event would likely have been spread across a larger section of the forest, not simply restricted to a specific tree. Lastly, it may be helpful to observe if the candidate UPT is located in areas which were known to yield stone projectile points or other stone artifacts, such as small circular firepits that may have been used by the Ute Indians during their hunts or in the camp areas.

A recent UPT search of the Hayman Fire burn area, located in northern Teller County, showed promising signs that many old growth trees and UPTs had survived the devastating fire. One cannot help but wonder how old these UPT are and how much longer might they live? For them to be a UPT, they would need to be at least 150 to 300 years old. If you were to ask a Ute Indian, they might say that unless something or someone cuts short their natural 800 year lifespan (i.e., wild land forest fire, disease or a human who simply thinks the tree is blocking their view of Pikes Peak), these UPT cultivated by their native ancestors might live another 500 to 650 years.

Several hundred sacred Ute Prayer Trees have been found still thriving in counties throughout the Pikes Peak Region. Ute elders are returning to visit their sacred trees in Saguache, Alamosa, Archuleta, Custer, Park, Teller, El Paso and Douglas Counties, while other UPTs have been confirmed as far north as Eagle County. One fact remains; UPTs provide physical evidence of the vast territory the Ute traveled during their traditional migrations throughout the Shining Mountains. Among the heaviest concentrations of UPTs discovered thus far is in the Black Forest of north central El Paso County and the Fox Run Regional Park remains an ideal location for the public viewing.

UPTs Hike in Fox Run Park

Those who may be interested in inspecting some of these fascinating CMTs can travel by car north from Colorado Springs on I-25, then take the first exit north of the United States Air Force Academy at the Baptist Road exit. Driving east on Baptist Road from I-25 a distance of about four miles you begin to enter the Black Forest. On the left or north side of Baptist Road, just off the roadway, can be found 15-16 magnificent varieties of Ute Prayer Trees, all visible without even getting out of the car. Turn south at the stop sign on to Roller Coaster Road. In about an eighth of a mile on the west side of the road is the parking lot for one of the trailheads into the Fox Run Park. The trail is well-maintained year-round by the dedicated staff of the El Paso County Parks Department.

Trailmarker Tree, Tree One

From the parking lot walk west past the outdoor public restroom, along the footpath, then take the first trail off to the left. After walking across the little wooden step bridge turn immediately right.

Look along the dry creek that the bridge went over, approximately thirty yards and you can see the first Trailmarker Tree. Walk west up the bank of the now dry creek bed, about 40 paces, toward this leaning Trailmarker UPT pointing along the creek bed to the southeast.

Notice how the tree is bent once about fifteen feet from the ground at a thirty degree angle until it straightens. The primary trunk extends outward a few feet where it withered and died away. The secondary trunk, called the Leader, took over the trees pursuit of the necessary sunlight required to sustain itself and grow. At the bend is a horizontal ligature or tie-down indentation at the inside curve. Extending down along the topside of the bark, for 3-4 feet the bark has been peeled away in the distinctive pattern of the Ute Medicine Man. Noticing the top ceremonial first cut of the bark was made with a sharp edged implement, one may assume it was made with an ax. This allowed an opening for two wooden or rock wedges to be driven down the desired length of the trunk and at the bottom, the bark was torn away. This distinct peeled bark pattern repeats itself throughout the Shining Mountains of Colorado.

One of the confirming factors to positively identifying UPT is in observing or reading the nearby geographical terrain. This area of the Black Forest was once covered with natural springs and even today when the snow melts the creeks begin to channel water downhill. These tributaries flow into the Black Squirrel Creek then connect to Monument Creek near the U.S. Air Force Academy. From there other streams converge as they flow south and join Fountain Creek, then flow further south to the Arkansas River. The Arkansas runs primarily east and flows into the Mississippi River and ultimately their waters empty into the Gulf of Mexico. If one were to reverse this route to travel up these waterways they would eventually arrive back at this exact place. The UPTs would not only help guide but mark important locations.

Trailmarker Tree, Tree Two

As one examines the nearby terrain due north of this first UPT Trailmarker and looks across the narrow ravine, approximately 75 yards, another identical Trailmarker Tree with the same thirty degree angled trunk can be found. This is another important characteristic worth mentioning; where one UPT is located, it is well worth the effort to look around for another UPT, as they are often found in groups or clusters and often point in the same direction or possibly towards one another. Both of these trees are pointing exactly 150 degrees southeast.

Walk across the ravine approximately 65 paces to this second UPT Trailmarker Tree. Notice the primary trunk on the outside of the one bend about ten feet above the ground. What looks like a branch was the primary trunk that withered and died away once the secondary trunk took over, just like the first Trailmarker tree we studied. Notice the oval shape of the tree between the ground and the bend. This was caused when the tree adjusted its cellular structure to better support the weight of the tree that is no longer directly over the portion of the tree trunk coming out of the ground.

Just above the ground level, at about eighteen inches in height on the outside curve of the tree, you can see an old cut scar caused by an ax being driven horizontally in a downward direction several times into the thick trunk of the tree. This chop mark was followed by several upper cuts until the tree was notched about six inches in length, top to bottom. Notice that this is a distinctly different pattern then that observed on the first UPT still visible across the dry creek to the south. This cut was caused later, most likely not by a Ute. When the tree was modified by the Ute it would have been too small to sustain this type of cut without killing the tree. This might be a good example of what is referred to as a blaze. To blaze is the term that applies to the act by the person who marks a trail. The blaze is also the mark that is left on the tree. The person who marks the trail are known as a trailblazer.

Walking west from this second Trailmarker tree along the main trail, several other curved or bent trees can be seen. Follow the trail uphill a few hundred yards, paralleling Baptist Road on your right until you come to a clearing in the trees. You will come to an informative sign erected by the El Paso County Park staff that takes care of Fox Run Park. This modern day Trailmarker identifies the Native Americans who used this area to hunt including the Ute, Cheyenne, Sioux and Arapahoe Tribes and generally describes the Clovis era. Unfortunately, this sign fails to point out the interesting UPT Burial Tree located about thirty yards to the northeast.

Burial Tree, Tree Three

Walk thirty yards northeast from the modern trailmarker regarding the Native Americans. This particular Burial Tree has several distinct features worth a closer look to include very discernible tie-down or ligature marks which are clearly visible on the inside of the second ninety degree bend of the trunk. Along the top of the trunk of the bend, a cut extends from about half way down the trunk, toward the first bend closer to the ground. The cut is old and expands as it nears the first bend. On the outside of the bend, a small amount of wood has been removed. This was done to sever the wood fibers to help keep the tree bent forward. As with other classic Ute Burial Trees, this Ponderosa tree would have been modified or cultivated to recognize one specific member of the Ute band.

The direction the tree points, in this case to the northeast, is significant as it denotes some long forgotten story about this beloved member of the Ute band, either where they died, were buried or perhaps where they were born. The direction of this and all Ute Indian Prayer Trees is not random: it is meaningful. There is or was, a purpose for the stake being driven in the ground at that particular point directing the tree to grow. When Colorado was a Territory, Teller County was part of the original El Paso County. In Teller County most of the UPTs point toward Pikes Peak. In the Black Forest area many of the UPTs and Trailmarker trees point to water sources, springs, trails, specific locations and Burial Trees.

Return to the modern Trailmarker sign on the trail. Notice the trail forks ahead to allow the option of continuing further west (where many UPTs of various varieties can be found) but for this tour, turn south, left, to see the next tree. Walk about 60-80 yards (90 paces) along the trail then look on the left (south) side of the trail on a hillside is the first of several remarkable UPTs.

Story or Ceremonial Trees, Trees Four and Five

The closest tree is one of two extraordinarily twisted, deformed looking Ponderosa Pines. Neither is overly tall. This UPT and the one 15 yards further to the south have multiple bends to the trunk and several limbs with peeled bark. The first UPT has evidence of burn scars consistent with other Ute Ceremonial Trees.

It can be suggested this tree was struck by lightning; however, examining further up the tree does not reveal the distinctive downward spiral pattern of a lightning strike, and you will notice something else. At about eye-level, a large beach ball size growth protrudes out from the trunk. This bulbous looking burl is almost certainly man-caused and, like the tree, very old.

A close examination of the second of what are believed to be either Ute Story or Ceremonial Trees shows a similar pattern of distortion that is clearly not natural. This second tree displays, on the inside curve of several bends, multiple unmistakable ligature or tie-down marks that clearly could not have been done all at one time. These trees required multiple modifications, over a period of cultivation that no doubt took years, if not generations to accomplish.

Don't examine these two trees without careful consideration of the larger geographical terrain of the immediate area. These two trees are situated between the old trail to the west, barracked on the east by a rocky knoll, and what would have been the headwaters of a now dry spring, what would have served as a minor tributary flowing to a larger creek then ultimately into the Arkansas River, etc. By traversing this route from the Mississippi River remaining on the left bank, directed by Trailmarker Trees or cairns of stacked rock where trees are not available, one arrives at this or dozens of other specific locations within the Black Forest.

Trailmarkers and Burial Tree, Trees Six, Seven and Eight

Walk another twenty yards southwest, downhill, there are a series of three large old UPTs consisting of two Trailmarker Trees and in the middle a Burial Tree. There is a green memorial park bench in view of this area. Taking in the old Trailmarker Tree on the east or left along the dry creek bed (tree furthest from the bench), notice it points uphill to the northeast towards another Trailmarker Tree at the top of the rise on the right (tree closest to the bench). Standing in front of this old Trailmarker Tree, closely examine a classic ligature tie-down mark at the inside of the curve.

Backtracking to the west towards the trail 20 yards it is worth stopping to examine the Burial Tree (between the two Trailmarker trees) with the two distinct ninety degree turns and the trunk running along the top of the ground pointing east. The tree displays the ligature marks and at the first bend, some of the fiber from the trunk was also removed similar to the first Burial Tree examined higher up the trail.

The Trailmarker tree closest to the bench is perhaps one of the oldest UPTs in the park other than what we will call the Grandmother Tree, possibly in all of the Black Forest. This huge old full-orange Ponderosa is positioned directly on the east edge of the trail and is directing the traveler uphill towards the east to the next tree higher up, the Burial Tree, and on up and over this divide. The old Trailmarker Tree is estimated to be 350 to 450 years old.

This old Trailmarker Tree provides a great bench to rest upon, a place to meet, to share a story or today a backdrop for a great photo opportunity. While studying this Trailmarker Tree or any one individual possible CMT or UPT, it is important to examine it as one piece to a much larger puzzle. In trying to determine if any Ponderosa in Fox Run Park or anywhere in the Pikes Peak Region is a UPT and what variety of UPT it is, one must try to read the role each candidate UPT may have played on the larger stage back in history.

Here, in this short hike, we have noted eight UPTs including four Trailmarkers, two Burial Trees, and a pair of Story Trees that collectively tell a story that reveals a piece of the Ute culture. These sacred trees tell of the history of the indigenous people, the Ute, who lived here and migrated through this forest where we stand today.

Story Tree - The Grandmother Tree, Tree Nine

Continue south down the trail where you can discover many more UPTs along both sides of the trail, including a Trailmarker off to the east side of the trail which unfortunately has died within the last few years. From the bench, this dead tree is approximately 150 paces on the left down the trail. According to the Ute beliefs this standing dead tree still contains the prayers offered around it by their Tribal Ancestors and should be treated with respect while being preserved until it is reclaimed by Mother Earth.

As you continue down the trail, it forms a T. When you reach the T you will see another Trailmarker tree with ligatures on the left. The trail to the left will bring you back to the parking lot at the trailhead. Take the right fork of the trail and be rewarded in a few hundred yards with the Grandmother Tree standing next to a memorial park bench. The tree was referred to as the Grandmother Tree by others interested in CMT that have hiked with me. The respectful name reflects the age of the tree. When the Ute went on this hike they felt the name was appropriate as her story could be a grandmother with arms outstretched embracing her children.

Prophecy Tree - The Portal Trees, Trees Ten and Eleven

There are two ways to get to the next two trees, one requires leaving the path, but is the easiest way to locate these unusual trees. Stand in back of the park bench near the Grandmother tree. Face the opposite way from the way the bench faces and stand in the center of the bench. Walk

110 paces up the hill in the direction you are facing which is a little south of due west. On the left you will see two trees that have been modified to form a living sculpture. One looks like a goal post at the end of an American football field. What story this UPT offered the Ute can only be speculated, but we know from research Don Wells and his team has done in Georgia with the Cherokee Indians, that the Cherokee used trees shaped similar to this goal post tree to mark territorial boundaries. The second tree in this sculpture creates a V shape with the first tree forming what looks like a Portal. We have named it the Portal tree just as a way of identification. We do not know what the Ute called this tree. Walking through the Portal heading west, to the top of the hill Pikes Peak comes into view at the top of the ridge.

The second way to approach the Portal Trees would be continue following the trail from the Grandmother tree. This way is longer but requires less cross country. When you get to the top of the ridge, with Pikes Peak on your right, look for a ravine on your left. Look east at the ravine and keeping the ravine on the right, the V of the Portal tree can be seen about 25 yards downhill. It is harder to find this way.

Examining the Portal Tree closely reveals two separate trees. One tree looks like branches that extend outward then upward forming a goal post looking tree. Others say it more resembles a person extending their arms outward to flex their bicep muscles. Looking closely at the southern branch where it comes in contact with the trunk of the second tree about eight feet from the ground, you can see where it has become fused or grown into the other tree. As you approach these two trees from below the untrained eye may not notice at the bottom of the tree trunk on the left where the bark has been peeled away. This peeled bark pattern is consistent with the peeled bark removal pattern of the Ute Medicine Man or Woman who struck the tree trunk at the top with a sharp implement, then drove two wooden or stone wedges down the length of the tree and tore the bark off at the bottom. The portion of bark removed is about twenty-four inches in length but much wider than most other bark removal patterns. Many cradle boards were made from peeled bark such as the size of the bark removed from this tree.

During a hike with Ruth Spencer, one of the organizers of the annual Ute picnic at Fox Run Park hosted Gleneagle Women's Club, Ruth posed an intriguing question when she asked why it is a person could walk right past these amazing Ute Prayer Trees and fail to notice them. Ruth was correct once you have been shown what to look for you begin to see them right away. She then offered a very insightful answer to her own question when she said, *"Do you think we can't see the trees for the forest?"* I think Ruth was spot on, until we have trained our eye to know what to look for all we see are trees in a forest.

Because of my interest in these trees, I have led numerous groups, including groups of Ute, on this hike through Black Forest. The Ute immediately understand the sacred trees, but others when first introduced to UPTs have felt that it is too far-fetched to believe that these trees were modified by Ute and not just flukes in nature. That is perfectly understandable. Most people when first introduced to this relatively unknown subject would also find many of these assertions somewhat unbelievable. Even I would have had difficulty in accepting everything at face-value at the beginning of my research. But the more we studied these trees and researched them, the more we appreciated them. I saved one of my favorite trees for last, the Prophecy Tree that those that have gone on this hike call the Hugging Tree.

Prophecy Tree – The Hugging Tree, Tree Twelve

What is believed to be a rare Prophecy Tree stands deep in the Forest to the southeast of the Portal Tree, northeast of the ponds located near the center of the park. From the Portal tree walk west beside the ravine on your left till you find the main trail. Take this trail to the left and head down the trail till you find a T. Take a left at the T and walk down the trail till you see the information signs that talk about tree fungus. Following the trail go approximately 25 paces from the trail signs. There is another trail barely visible on the left facing east. Follow this trail east for approximately 140 paces. You will notice a very unusual UPT and a barbed wire fence to the right. There is not a foot path or regular trail that leads beyond this location. There are Trailmarker trees that point the way. With the barbed wire fence to your right, about 25 feet from the fence, follow the fence line downhill another 210 paces and look for the tall hugging tree on your left.

This location may have been one of the most sacred places in all the Black Forest. Standing here are two remarkable intertwined Ponderosa pine trees that are estimated to be three to four hundred years old. One of the trees is slightly smaller than the other and leans into the larger tree at a distance of about 18-20 feet in the air and literally wraps its branches around the other tree in what appears to be a loving embrace. A closer inspection of where these two trees physically join together reveals how the bark of the larger tree was split downward so that the other tree could fuse into the trunk of the larger. Even the smaller branches of the tree reaching around the other appear to resemble shoulders and at the end of the branches the outer limbs look like fingers.

Some speculate these two trees resemble two lovers, locked in an eternal loving embrace or possibly a child hugging a parent or grandparent. Absorbing the nature around you, the tranquility of this sacred place is unmistakable. The person who was with me when this discovery was made, Phil Tinsley, remarked at the time how the trees resemble the spires of a church and how this place feels like a cathedral.

We may never know what prophecy this living sculpture was meant to convey or if the prophecy has occurred or is yet to be. What is unmistakable is the awareness that this place under these trees was and remains a sacred place. This place, these trees must be protected and preserved for future generations, most especially future generations of the Ute Nation. The Ute were guided by the sun, the stars, the mountains, the waterways and of course their sacred trees. The people who applied their special skills and knowledge to modify these Ute Prayer Trees have "walked on" as the Ute say, but many of their sacred trees remain yet to be discovered.

The next time you find yourself driving down a tree-lined road in the Shining Mountains of Colorado or hiking along a secluded tree-covered trail in the forest and notice an unusually distorted, bent or twisted tree, who knows, maybe you have discovered something very old and historic and sacred. You may have discovered a Ute Indian Prayer Tree.

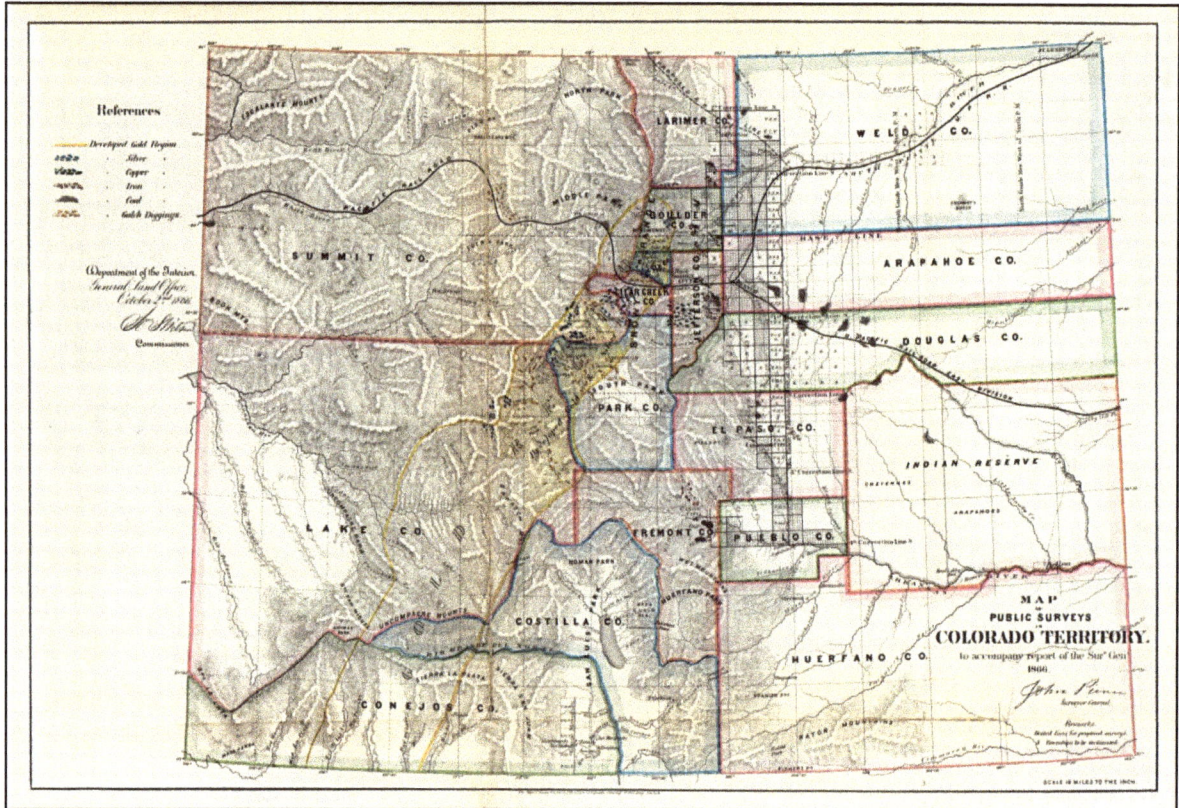

1866 US GLO CT Map: This early map of the Colorado Territory (CT) was commissioned by the United States Department of the Interior (DOI) Government Land Office (GLO). The map is of "Public Surveys in Colorado Territory" and released "to accompany report of the Sur Gen 1866" under Commissioner J.S. Wilson and signed by John Pinner (sp) Surveyor General. It indicates the boundaries for original 17 counties of the Colorado Territory, including El Paso County (which at the time incorporated all of today's Teller County). This historic map captures a time before there were any major roads. There is a fascinating trail represented by a dotted line that connects several counties and follows much of what is known of the old Indian trails. Pikes Peak (Pk) is depicted in the mountains of western El Paso County and the town of Colorado City (established in 1859) is shown with Fountaine que Brulle (today's Fountain Creek) running through the center of town. Two of the three routes that led to the 1859-1861 Pikes Peak Gold Rush, the Santa Fe Trail to the south and Smoky Hills Trail to the north, crossed over this Indian Reserve (the Oregon Trail was further north). Bent's Old Fort and Bent's (new) Fort are shown to the south of the Indian Reserve along the Arkansas. The Ute Territory was generally accepted as being the western one-third of the Colorado Territory. In the upper left corner the legend outlines the primary cause for the loss of land granted to the Ute people - the Developed Gold Region. This Developed Gold Region, which also listed the location of silver, copper, iron and coal, along with the gulch (gold) diggings, was known as the Mineral Belt and ran right through the heart of the Ute's Shining Mountains. This US GLO map is in the public domain.

Chapter 5 - First Contact, the Ute Nation
(1492-1637)
There is no rich, no poor;
I can only be rich if I am known to possess many friends.

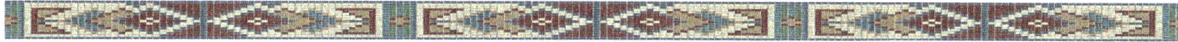

While most educators credit Christopher Columbus as discovering America, most historians acknowledge there were earlier explorers. There is convincing evidence to confirm the Vikings traversed across the northern Atlantic and arrived in the New World some 500 years before Columbus. Even before the Norsemen the Polynesians, Chinese and Japanese may have sailed across the vast Pacific Ocean to explore the west coasts of North and South America. Some historians even suggest the Phoenicians, an ancient maritime trading culture that spread outward from the Mediterranean from 1550 BC to 300 BC, could have found the New World long before Columbus' discovery. Ute Elders will tell you they knew where it was all along.

The time before any written historical account is generally referred to as pre-history or pre-historic and the time before Columbus' well-documented discovery is known as pre-Columbian. Columbus who had started out seeking a trade route to the West Indies made his inadvertent discovery of the New World on October 12th, 1492. Columbus was an Italian born explorer but claimed the New World for Spain as they had financed his expedition. Columbus was the first to refer to the people he encountered as Indians, whom he thought were the people from the Indies, a mistaken choice of labels. Unfortunately, not even the native people Columbus encountered had a name to refer to themselves collectively, so the name Columbus gave them remains today. Columbus would make a total of four voyages to the New World and would return with many, perhaps numbering in the hundreds, Native Americans enslaved in bondage.

On Columbus' second voyage in 1493, he would reintroduce the horse to North America for the use of the Spanish, after an absence of at least 12,000 years. Archaeological evidence supports the theory that North America had been home to at least three distinct varieties; including a much smaller horse, another about the same size as the Pinto favored by the Ute and a larger draft horse, similar in size to today's massive Clydesdales. During the last Ice Age, approximately 10,000 B.C., many horses were believed to have crossed east to west and northward over the Bearing Straits into Asia and Europe before the glacial melts caused the seas to rise isolating North and South America.

Christopher Columbus in 1498 after returning from his third of four voyages to the New World said: "I have come to believe that this is a mighty continent which was hitherto unknown... Your Highnesses have an Other World here." The myth that Native Americans, prior to the time of Columbus' arrival, were simply small wandering bands of native people scattered aimlessly about this vast untouched wilderness was not correct. Nothing could be further from the truth. The Ute, as were other tribes, were nomadic, traveling with the seasons for hunting, gathering and wintering, but their traditions vast and their culture rich.

One of the best sources today to document this pre-Columbian period in the Americas is the book by Charles C, Mann, *1491 New Revelations of the Americas Before Columbus*. Mann offers an extraordinary look into the various cultures of the millions of people who lived on the North American Continent for tens of thousands of years before Columbus ever waded ashore in 1492. The book argues a combination of recent findings in different fields suggests that Native population in the western hemisphere was more numerous. The Natives were in America much earlier and they had a more sophisticated culture that controlled and shaped the natural landscape much more than previously thought.

Today we better understand and accept the existence of a vast Native Trail System across this continent, partially lined with Native American Trailmarker Trees. This trail system seems to have extended across the Pikes Peak Region with some of the trail networks in the Shining Mountains almost serving as the hub to a wheel. Directional Trailmarker Trees extend not only throughout the Shining Mountains, but as far north into what is today British Columbia in northwest Canada.

The study of ancient seafaring cultures clearly demonstrates that many pre-Columbian people had advanced shipbuilding skills to not only build a seaworthy craft capable of traveling great distances, but the navigational ability to not only take them where they wanted to go but to return them safely back home again. Advanced tools and techniques for shipbuilding and navigation would likely have spread across oceans and waterways between trading people and blending cultures.

What are known today as the Five Civilized Tribes were the first Native Americans to have contact with Europeans. They would assimilate many of the cultural and technological practices of the early European American settlers. These tribes were the Choctaw, Creek, Seminole, Cherokee and Chickasaw. The Ute would come into contact much later with the Europeans. The Ute, divided into seven nomadic tribes, lived in what is now Utah and Colorado. They too were influenced by the Spanish, who introduced them to the horse, or as the Ute believe, re-introduced them to the horse.

Longevity of Ute in the Shining Mountains

If you ask the Nuche (Ute Indians) how long they have lived in the Shining Mountains, they will tell you they have always lived there since the beginning of time. In addition to the Ute's oral history lacking a migration story, their Creation Story teaches them that the Creator created the earth first and then the animals. When he finished creating all the animals, they all spoke a language where they could understand one another. Lastly, he created the People and placed them in a bag which he handed to his young brother with directions to place them in the Shining Mountains. When his brother opened the bag due to curiosity, many People escaped, the ones that did not escape, the Ute, were rewarded by being placed in the Shining Mountains. The Ute hold the steadfast belief that they are all related and all come from the same Creator.

Interestingly enough recent DNA analysis that was conducted by the University of California indicated that Native American genealogy is one of the most unique in the world. An international team of researchers found a unique variant of a genetic marker in the DNA samples from modern day Native American and Eurasian groups. Their conclusion seems to support a single ancestral population theory linking Native Americans, Greenlanders and western Beringians, as being derived from a common ancestor which had been isolated from the rest of the Asian continent for thousands of years prior to a migration to the Americas.

Dennis O'Rourke of the University of Utah theorizes that land called Beringia, now submerged, had a climate and resources that could sustain humans for thousands of years. Found in the area of the Bering Strait, Beringia allowed the passage from Asia to Alaska then to the rest of North America. Is it not equally plausible this DNA analysis could support a reverse migration out of the Americas? If nothing else, the DNA study seems to support the teachings passed down by the Ute Elders that they are related to other Native Americans.

It is fairly well accepted that the Ute belong to the Numic speakers, a Uto-Aztecan language that include the Paiute, Hopi, Comanche and Shoshone. Some historians suggest the Ute migrated with other Numic speakers from the west coast approximately 800 years ago. However, the Ute believe they are descendants of the original inhabitants of today's Colorado, and most all historians agree with the Ute, that they lived here longer than anyone else.

Archaeological discoveries have helped us understand how long humans have lived in what was known as Ute Territory. Since the Pleistocene period when the ancestors of the Ute hunted the large animals like the mammoth and mastodon, before they all became extinct, the Ute always considered themselves big game hunters. The legends of these hunters and their massive prey would have been told and retold around the campfires of the indigenous people for generations. The Ute also retained history through CMTs. One peculiar tree discovered in northern El Paso County has what appears to be a trunk and two parallel tusks. Could this CMT, likely a UPT, possibly be a story tree cultivated long ago to help the tribal elders convey the oral history of these giant mammoths to their tribal youth?

There have been several mastodon and mammoth fossils recovered up and down Colorado's Front Range including an important site discovered in 1932 near Dent, Colorado (east of Loveland), in Weld County. The Dent Site documented the discovery of the first projectile point in mammoth ribs. The projectile point was determined to be Clovis (10,000 BCE) predating the Folsom Points and is presently located in the Denver Museum of Nature and Science. This finding was historic in that it was one of the first pieces of direct evidence of human interaction establishing that man and mammoth coexisted in the Americas.

Perhaps the most advanced projectile points used for either arrowheads or the larger spear points, were named after the city near where they were first located, Clovis, New Mexico, in 1929. Clovis points were crafted using a technique known as bifacial percussion or pressure flaking and were applied alternatively along both edges of the flat projectile point creating a very thin blade. This technique is what helps identify a Clovis point by these very distinct shallow groves at the base called flutes. These indentations are carved or flaked at the base where the stone projectile point would have been attached or hafted to the wooden arrow or spear, by what is sometimes referred to as a foreshaft.

The first Clovis projectile points were dated to 13,500 B.C. and unearthed in association with fossilized Columbian Mammoth skeletal remains. Some Clovis projectile points have been found to have been fashioned out of obsidian, a glass-like stone that when flaked off or knapped, produces an extremely shape edge. The edge of an obsidian stone is so sharp that it is still in used today as a surgical instrument. There have been many Clovis projectile points discovered in the Pikes Peak Region of El Paso and Teller Counties.

Located approximately two hundred and twenty miles north of the Clovis discovery lies Folsom, another major site for projectile points situated near the Kiowa National Grasslands near Folsom, New Mexico. The Folsom Point is dated between 9500 BC and 8000 BC, and they have also been found in the Ute's Shining Mountains, most notably at a site known as Mountain Ridge, west of Gunnison, Colorado. Folsom projectile points were also produced by flintknapping a stone tool, identified by the conchoidal fracturing of the edges of the stone tool fashioning it into the desired shape of a leaf-like appearance with a fluted base. They are generally broader in width and somewhat thicker than Clovis points. A few of the Clovis and Folsom points found in Colorado are believed to pre-date those found in Clovis or Folsom, New Mexico.

The American Mastodon was believed to have gone extinct towards the end of the Paleolithic era approximately 10,000-12,000 years ago, which allows for an overlap of several thousand years where these huge American Mastodons and slow-moving woolly Columbian Mammoths roamed the Rocky Mountain Front Range with the indigenous peoples. Archaeological evidence found in northern El Paso County at what appears to have been an ancient hunting camp produced four Clovis Projectile Points (three arrowheads and one spear point) and estimated to be approximately 10,000 years old. When coupled with the carbon dating of a nearby fire pit, estimated to be 13,000 years old, these stone tools add to the confirmation that the ancient native peoples in what is today the Pikes Peak Region may have collaborated in large group hunts for these massive animals.

In an interview with Dr. James A. Goss, a recognized authority of Ute history and culture by the

Ute elders, with Cathy Wright at the Colorado Springs Fine Arts Center on August 18th, 1999 in regards to the Center's research on the Ute, Dr. Goss shared how he came to live on the Southern Ute Reservation with his wife and children for three years, learning the Ute language, and culture and traditions, and capturing the stories of the elders. He shared how the Ute tradition mandates that since they were created in the Shining Mountains, they have an obligation to be in the right place at the right time to be good stewards of the resources, which includes the plants and the animals. Their view was that the land owned them, as opposed to the Ute owning the land. Dr. Goss acknowledged how other historians disagree with the Ute traditions regarding their belief that they have always been in the Shining Mountains since the beginning of time. Dr. Goss believes the burden of proof isn't upon the Ute people, but upon those who claim the Ute oral history is mistaken.

Dr. Goss does discuss during his interview a point of view shared by many archaeologists known as the Numic spread. This theory suggests, "That the ancestors of the Ute and the Paiutes and the Shoshones and the Comanche spread out recently over the Great Basin from the southwest corner in southeastern California or something like that. But that gets into a complex model that will probably ultimately won't be as convincing as the model that the ancestors of these people have been here for 10,000 years." Dr. Goss goes on to share how the Uto-Aztecans were also the ancestors of the Ute, as well as the Aztecs of Mexico who have a tradition of migrating from the north from a place of many waters.

Dr. Goss went on to discuss a word in the Ute language for a spiritual leader, póo-gat, which is a derivative of the Ute word for road, póo or the way. The póo-gat is the "one that knows the way" who are generally the tribal elders. When you are on the road to spiritual enlightenment, you are following the way of the elders, the ones who know the way in which you want to go, for they have been there before. Just as important to the survival of the Ute in knowing where to go to hunt was when to go. Dr. Goss described as an example how the Muache Ute had their Bear Dance in the area around Conejos in southern Colorado on the west side of the San Luis Valley.

Dr. Goss explained, "The Bear Dance authorized them (the Muache Utes) to move higher up into the mountains and they would move on up into South Park, up here from Colorado Springs. In the fall, that group would traditionally come down Ute Pass, and camp in places like the Garden of the Gods or Manitou Springs or along Camp Creek that ran south downward in front of the Garden of the Gods. Then the group would kind of split up; the men and a few of the women would go off onto the plains a little further and hunt buffalo while the elderly and the children would keep close to the mountains and harvest piñon nuts along the Front Range. Then they would move south along the eastern side of the Sangre de Cristos and then back into winter camp."

Dr. Goss continued to write, "This was the pattern before they had horses, but the main thing you can say about this was when the horses came, that gave them more mobility and they could expand it a little more. They could get more people together in a group, and they could carry more household goods, and they could start dragging the tepees along with them and things like that. That, obviously, they couldn't do when they were just on foot." Dr. Goss shared the Ute, "were very aware of the movement of the sun, and the changing of the seasons. The Vernal Equinox, Summer Solstice, Autumn Equinox and the Winter Solstice all told them when they needed to be moving towards the Spring Resource Camps, Summer Hunting Camps, Autumn Pinyon and Hunting Camps or hunkering down for the Winter Camps in the Basins."

The Ute, First Contact with Europeans and Horses

The 1500s were a time of great exploration in the Americas which would bring the Europeans to their first contact with the Ute. Early Spanish and then later French explorers traveled waterways into the new lands. It is widely known that Trailmarker Trees from various tribes lined many of the waterways providing direction to inlets or tributaries or crossings.

One impact the Spanish had on the Ute was the horse and its impact on Ute culture. Before the horse, the Ute carried or dragged their possessions from camp to camp using a travois, which were long poles used to construct tepees often pulled by large dogs. Dogs were revered by the Ute and were also used for hunting, camp defense by alerting them to approaching danger and in lean times, a dog, like the horse, could be eaten to sustain the tribe. Ute trails were often discernible by two parallel grooves in the earth caused by dragging the travois along the paths that had been traveled by the Ute for centuries before the arrival of the Europeans.

To the Native Americans the single most prized possession the Conquistadors brought with them from Spain was the horse, although it was against Spanish law to allow natives to acquire the horse. Accounts do say horses did escape and go wild, but when they became part of native culture is unknown. The first known written account of natives of the Americas having acquired horses was in 1637 when Spanish Governor of New Spain, Luis de Rosas, headquartered in Santa Fe, recorded a journal entry regarding a battle between his mounted troops and a band of mounted Ute. Later, in 1680 the Pueblo Indians, under the leadership of Chief Pope, revolted and drove the Spanish out of Santa Fe, many horses were left behind and possession was taken by the Pueblo Indians. In the late 1600s it is noted that the Pueblo Indians did ride well, but mainly valued the horse for food and as a item for trade.

Historians differ on how the Ute acquired the horse. One account mentions Ute being enslaved by the Spanish who forced them to work in the silver mines the Spanish were digging in the Northern Territory. This story tells how 80 Ute were taken into captivity, while an unknown number were killed. These Ute slaves were forced to work in the Spanish silver mines then escaped and took with them the horse herd.

Other historians suggest horses were not simply stolen, but taken by force, possibly during a battle. A petroglyph attributed to the Ute, known as the Wolfe Ranch Arches in Utah, illustrates early Ute mounted on horses. It is believed to be dated from the 1600-1800s and appears to teach how horses and dogs were used to help the Ute hunt sheep. Another important Native American petroglyph which may be attributed to the Ute is located about 350 miles west of La Junta, near Olathe, Colorado. This petroglyph is a historically significant documented case on record showing the Ute Indians mounted on horseback.

When the Ute acquired the horse, the tribes were changed forever. With the acquisition of the horse, the distance a tribe could cover and the speed at which they could travel dramatically increased. Their ability to defend themselves or to hunt larger game, especially the bison, substantially improved the influence and survivability of the tribe. On the other side, with expansion of the Ute's hunting grounds came the need to protect those hunting domains.

The Ute would become very accomplished at breeding horses and went on to refine the Spanish Pinto capable of enduring the high trails interwoven through the Shining Mountains. To the Ute the number of horses a man possessed was not a matter of personal possessions or an indication of individual wealth. The number of horses a Ute man had under his control told of the value he could provide his tribe. It showed how much food could be carried with them to help sustain the tribe though the winter.

There are written accounts that survive from the late 15th and 16th Centuries that describe how the routes the Ute established were used by other Native American tribes and the Europeans. What became known as the Old Spanish Trail trampled over by Alvar Nunez Caveza de Vaca (1488-1558) and Juan de Onate (1550-1630), were actually old Ute trails that had been used for many centuries before the arrival of the earliest of the Spanish explorers. One early contact the Spanish explorers made while pushing northward, up the Rio Grande River, was with an Indian encampment in the San Luis Valley, directly south of today's Colorado New Mexico border. The expedition leader, Juan de Onate wrote in his report back to the Spanish Crown, "The Indians are numerous in all that land, they always follow the cattle (bison) and kill them at the first shot with the greatest skill, while ambushed in brush blinds made at watering places."

It may never be known how long the Ute lived in the Rocky Mountains. The Ute of today believe they are the descendants of the original inhabitants of Colorado, and most historians agree the Ute lived here longer than other tribes. When the Europeans first arrived in what is today Colorado the Ute were already there. The Spanish called the Ute the Sky Blue People or the People of the Shining Mountains.

The impact upon the Ute culture following their First Contact with Europeans during the 17th Century seems to coincide with estimated age of their older culturally modified trees which are thought to be around 350-450 years old. As the distances the Ute could travel during their annual migration routes doubled or tripled, so too grew their need for an expanded trail system, one that would become lined by Ute Trailmarker Trees. The bond that formed between the Ute and the horse

Southern Ute CC Tutt: This rare old photograph is believed to have been previously unpublished and was discovered in the Abby L. Kernochan (1917-1979) Photo Album #8 p. 1, by Curator Jessy Randall, of the Special Collections, Tutt Library, Colorado College, Colorado Springs, Colorado. The photo is cataloged as "Band of Ute, San Juan Region" and the photographer is identified as W.J. Carpenter. The photo shows twelve Ute men, seven of whom are mounted on horseback. There is a faint inscription in the lower left hand corner, which has faded over time; however it is believed this photo may have been taken at the old Los Pinos Agency in Saguache County, Colorado. The Los Pinos Indian Agency was established pursuant to the Treaty of 1868 to keep peace within the Ute boundaries and distribute treaty goods to the Tabeguache Ute. There is what appears to be a white man standing in the background near the corner of a two story wooden framed building who may be the Indian Agent. The Ute man standing, second from the right, is wearing what appears to be a tribal police badge and when the photo was shown to Southern Ute Tribal Elder, Dr. James Jefferson, he replied, "Hey, that's my Grandfather! That's Severo." Severo was a highly respected Southern Ute Elder and sub-chief under Chief Ouray (1833-1880). This photo is undated however it is believed to have been taken in the early 1870's at the Los Pinos Agency, which did have a sawmill (note the hand-hewn logs on the older building to the right and the cut lumber on the building that was added-on and the two story building in the background). The Los Pinos Agency was relocated a short distance away in 1875 and was used by Chief Ouray to mount the rescue efforts for the Meeker women and children abducted during what became known as the Meeker Massacre. This photo is published courtesy of the Special Collections, Tutt Library, Colorado College.

Northern Ute PPLD: This photo is from the Special Collections Digital Photo Archives of the Pikes Peak Library District (PPLD), Colorado Springs, Colorado. This photo is identified as Image Number 001-295, Collection Number MSS-0001 and is titled as, "Ute Indians Near Meeker, Colorado." The photographer is listed as unknown and the photo description is written as follows; "Two Ute Indians in front of tipi in valley with mountain behind. Horse is tied in background. Fringed, beaded bag and other belongings are piled to the left of the tipi." Photo identified on back as "Near Meeker, Colo. Back of Charles Fox Gardiner's home in Meeker, Colo. Ute Camp. Friends of his - 1884." The photo was cataloged as "Northern Ute women with tipi" and is believed to have been taken near the White River Reservation. The photo was from the Margaretta M. Boas Photograph Collection and is believed to have been previously unpublished. Of interest is the intricate beadwork visible on the satchels near where the ponies are standing. The tipi covering appear to have been made from canvas, as opposed to animal hides, as was traditionally used until the mid to late nineteenth century. This photo is published courtesy of Special Collections, Pikes Peak Library District.

Ute Mountain Ute (PPLD): This rare photo was located by Dennis Daily, Assistant Manager, in the Special Collections of the Pikes Peak Library District (PPLD), Colorado Springs, Colorado. The photo is ca. 1892, the year the H. Jay Smith Exploring Party traveled through the Four Corners area of Colorado collecting materials from the Cliff Dwellers culture from what is now Mesa Verde. Included in the Exploration Party were artist Alexis Fournier and an unknown photographer. The Exploring Party was collecting Native American artifacts for a major exhibition that would be mounted at the World's Columbian Exposition in Chicago (1892-1893). Richard Wetherill and another cowboy from Mancos, Charlie Mason, were the first two white men to discover the Cliff Palace in what became known as Mesa Verde. H. Jay Smith and his partner C.D. Hazzard purchased a huge number of artifacts from Richard Wetherill and his family. Richard Wetherill later operated a photography business which specialized in views of the Cliff Dwellings and other ruins. The Smith/Hazzard collection of Native American artifacts number around 10,000 pieces and was purchased by the University of Pennsylvania in the early part of the 20th Century. The Ute man standing first from the left is wearing a cartridge belt and the man sitting second from the right is wearing a tribal police badge. Several of the Ute are wearing or carrying beautiful blankets which might suggest they were affiliated with the Capote band; however, the Weminuche band were known to be more concentrated in the Mesa Verde area especially after 1896 when they broke away to organize the Ute Mountain Ute Reservation. The second man standing from the left is wearing what appears to be a freshly wrapped bandage on his left hand. The Photographer is thought to be H. Jay Smith and is hand signed and numbered 900 with the title stamped in the lower left corner "Exploring Party." This photo is published courtesy of the Special Collections, Pikes Peak Library District.

Chapter 6 - The Ute
The People of Shining Mountains (1638-1860)
Sunwise is Right Thinking, know where it is you stand,
life is a circle, share the chant.

The culture of the Ute varied somewhat from one geographical region to the next, depending on what natural resources the Creator provided them on the prairies, deserts, wetlands, grasslands or in the mountains. As with other Native tribes, the Ute culture evolved over time from one generation to the next as they were impacted by the influence of other cultures and technologies.

As the Ute moved across their timeworn trails through the Shining Mountains from one season to the next, they were guided as much by the sun and the stars as they were by the changes in the weather. They were very aware of the hibernation patterns of animals and when it was time to harvest food to sustain them through the long winter. The well-worn trails of the Ute traversed over mountain passes, across arid deserts and along the rivers and their tributaries. How long the Ute were guided by their Trailmarker Trees may never be known, but there is the possibility that the need to mark trails increased as their hunting domains expanded following the acquisition of the horse.

The Ute Indians were by nature a peaceful people; however, when conflict occurred with other tribes they were fierce warriors. Conflicts occurred with the Comanche, Arapahoe, Cheyenne, Sioux and Kiowa Indian tribes. The Ute lived in the mountains and high meadows and always preferred to fight from a defensive position. Their knowledge of the mountains allowed them high ground in a fight and the capability to hide from enemies. One story that survives relates how twelve Ute warriors were attacked by another tribe of over 200 hundred warriors. During the battle nine of the Ute were severely wounded or killed, but the Ute were able to withstand the attack until the other tribe finally gave up and left.

To many of the warring Indian Tribes, the purpose of battle was to kill the other warrior so they themselves could grow stronger by capturing the enemy's spirit along with possessions including their women and young children, whom they would often raise as their own. Although the Ute were known as fierce warriors especially when in defense of their tribe, they were first a welcoming people who showed compassion and a willingness to share their knowledge of how to survive and thrive in this land.

First Contact with Ute in the Shining Mountains

Early Europeans who traveled through Ute territory and wrote of their encounters with the Ute have helped historians today understand the Ute people. The first European contacts the

Ute encountered were made in Spanish Territory, likely just north of Santa Fe, founded by the Spanish in the early 1600s. The Spanish explorers in the 16th and 17th Centuries were among the first to document the names of the individual Ute bands and geographical territories which they seemed to control. Territorially speaking, the Ute controlled one of the largest land of any Native American tribe, extending from the San Juan River on the south, north to the Yampa River and from the base of the Rocky Mountains down along the Front Range, west over the Rocky Mountains all the way to directly south of Utah Lake. The reason the Ute were able to occupy this vast rugged terrain was due in part to the complex network of trails, guided along the way by their Ute Trailmarker Trees.

According to Dr. Jefferson, the Ute were one tribe until they were contacted by the white man who began to group them into geographical areas. The original Ute family bands were eventually classified into seven bands by the Spanish. Although the Ute were free to move from one tribal area to the next or from one Ute leader to the next.

Dr. Jefferson explained that to the Ute, the white man was anyone who was not Native American: white, black or yellow. In his book, The Southern Ute, A Tribal History, Dr. Jefferson writes, "The language of the Ute is Shoshonean which is a branch or a dialect of the Uto-Aztecan language. It is believed that the people who speak Shoshonean separated from other Uto-Aztecan speaking groups about the time of the birth of Christ. Other Indian groups of the U.S. who speak Shoshonean are the Paiutes, Goshutes, Shoshones, Bannocks, and some tribes in California."

"Eventually," Dr. Jefferson's book explains, "the Ute became concentrated into a loose confederation of seven bands." The names of the seven bands and the areas they lived in at the time the Ute were first contacted by the Spanish are, according to Dr. Jefferson's book, identified as follows:

1. Mouache – band lived in southern Colorado and in New Mexico almost down to Santa Fe (according to other historical sources, they also frequented the eastern slopes of the Rockies, from Denver as far south to near Las Vegas, New Mexico).

2. Capote – band inhabited the San Luis Valley in Colorado near the headwaters of the Rio Grande and in New Mexico especially around the region where the towns of Chama and Tierra Amarilla are now located (according to other historical sources, the Capote are sometimes known as the Caputa, and the word Capote is the name the Spanish gave this band who were known to wear distinctly woven coats or capes; a capote is the name for the embroidered capes worn by the Spanish bullfighter, the Matador).

3. Weeminuche – band occupied the valley of the San Juan River and its northern tributaries in Colorado and northwestern New Mexico (according to other historical sources, the name

is sometimes spelled Weenuche or Weenuchiu).

4. Tabeguache – band (also called Uncompahgre) lived in the valleys of the Gunnison and Uncompahgre Rivers in Colorado.

5. Grand River Ute – band (also called Parianuc) lived along the Grand River in Colorado and Utah.

6. Yampa – band (also known as the Yamparicas or White River Ute, according to other historical sources) inhabited the Yampa River Valley and adjacent land in northwestern Colorado.

7. Uintah Ute – band (sometimes spelled Uinta, according to other historical sources) inhabited the Uintah Basin, especially the western portion (and, according to other historical sources, eastern Utah).

Dr. Jefferson's book further states, "Of the bands mentioned above, the first two (Mouache and Capote) make up the present day Southern Ute with headquarters at Ignacio, Colorado. The Weeminuches are now called the Ute Mountain Ute with headquarters at Towaoc, Colorado. The last four mentioned (Tabeguache, Grand, Yampa, and Uintah) now comprise the Northern Ute on the Uintah-Ouray Reservation with headquarters at the town of Fort Duchesne, Utah."

"A long time ago, these seven groups of Ute were broken up into small family units for a large portion of each year. It was necessary to do this because food was scarce and it took a large area in the mountains to support a small number of people. Each family unit had to have a great deal of room since food-gathering couldn't be done so well in large groups. From early spring until late in the fall, these family units of Ute would hunt for deer, elk, antelope, and other animals; they would gather seeds of grasses, wild berries and fruits; occasionally they would plant corn, beans, and squash in mountain meadows and harvest them in the autumn."

As a forward to his exceptionally well-researched book, Across the Northern Frontier, Spanish Explorations in Colorado, Phil Carson wrote that on July 7th, 1694, New Mexico Governor Don Diego de Vargas wrote in his journal, "I left this place and took the road leading to the land of the Yuttas." In the chronology at the back of his book, Carson writes, "Governor Diego de Vargas obtains grain for starving settlers from Taos Pueblo, and then loops north to avoid ambush. He crosses the Rio Grande in Colorado's San Luis Valley and encounters friendly Ute." For 1705, Carson writes, "Comanches, brought by Ute, first appear at a Taos trade fair" and in another notation for 1719 he writes, "In pursuit of Comanches, Governor Antonio Valverde y Cosio crosses the Sangre de Cristo Mountains east of Taos and rides north up the Colorado's Front Range as far as today's Black Forest Divide" (today's Palmer Divide).

Trade fairs were sponsored by the Spanish yearly, allowing the Indians to bring goods to trade. A truce was called during the fair among the various tribes. The Ute brought furs, baskets and, as noted by the Spanish, hides that were of high quality. Although the fairs were peaceful, conflicts did occur between the Spanish and Native Americans. The Spanish pushed for illegal trade of slaves causing problems between tribes as it became more profitable to raid and take prisoners from one tribe and sell them to the Spanish. The Spanish government had laws that stated natives could not ride horses and no trading of horses, but the law was broken. Due to the law however; it was easier to obtain horses through raids on Spanish settlements. The Ute were involved in raids, but seldom killed when raiding. It was not a case of showing valor, but the necessity of taking items needed for the survival of the Ute.

Much of what we know of the Ute during the time that they first had encounters with the Europeans is one sided. As the Ute had no written language, what was written regarding the Ute was from the eyes of the early Europeans that had contact with the Ute.

Phil Carson's book mentions other references the Spanish noted with respect to contact with the Ute. In 1765 Governor Tomas Velez Cachupin sent Juan Maria Antonio de Rivera northwest up the Rio Chama to explore the Colorado River and to "seek tribes said to live beyond the Ute and also to prospect for silver in the mountain." Juan Maria de Rivera entered what is today Colorado near Pagosa Springs. Today we find this area rich with Ute Indian Prayer Trees many well over three hundred years old. De Rivera then traveled west to where Durango is presently located before turning north to where the Uncompahgre and Gunnison rivers converge before returning to Santa Fe. Rivera would lead eventually three more expeditions into Ute territory to trade with the Ute.

In 1776-77 two Franciscan priests, Atanasio Dominguez and Silvestre Velez de Escalante, along with a party of twelve, set out from Santa Fe in an attempt to establish a trading route to the missions in California. They traveled northwest up the Rio Chama across western Colorado and deep into Utah in search of a path to the Pacific Ocean. The two fathers were not only warmly greeted by the Ute but were guided along much of their route through what is today southwest Colorado and into eastern Utah before they ran out of provisions and turned back before facing the coming of winter. The priest noted that influential Ute were well mounted though many Ute had no horses at all. Traders continued to use this (Old Spanish Trail) route to reach the Ute.

In addition to the Spanish, French fur trappers also had early contact with the Ute Indians. The French followed the Arkansas River from its confluence with the mighty Mississippi River, upriver to the west in pursuit of the beaver, otter, bison and other fur bearing animals and often traded with the Ute. The French trapper's exploration led them to the base of a mountain peak (later named Pikes Peak) and to a creek with bubbling springs. They were so impressed with the springs that they named the creek Fountaine Qui Bouille meaning, The Boiling Fountain or Fountain that Boils (later shortened simply to Fountain Creek). The French encountered many indigenous people coming in peace to these sacred springs that naturally spewed water continuously 40 to 100 feet straight into the air. Here these people made offerings to their Creator, often leaving behind gemstones, ceremonial arrowheads or pieces of colored cloth or ribbon tied to the branches of nearby trees.

For the Spanish problems arose with the Comanche and would bring them closer to the Ute as their allies against the Comanche. A battle fought on September 26, 1768, at Ojo Caliente, claimed the life of Comanche War Chief Cuerno Verde, the elder (Green Horn was the name he was given by the Spanish). This violent conflict was finally won by the Spanish at the eastern foot of the 12,352 peak in the Wet Mountains of Colorado that today bears the Indian War Chief's son's name, Green Horn Mountain.

The fierce son of the Indian Chieftain was said to have worn his father's headdress adorned with a green horn into battle, possibly to distinguish himself or use as a bugle. Chief Cuerno Verde the younger inherited his father's name and the green horn he carried into battle against the Spanish. On September 3rd, 1779, he would also die in battle, killed by Spanish troops under the command of Governor Juan Bautista de Anza. His death occurred near the foot of Green Horn Mountain by present day Rye, Colorado. As was the case with Green Horn the elder, Governor de Anza's military expedition was also commissioned in response to Comanche Indians raiding farms and ranches, this time north of Santa Fe.

Juan Bautista de Anza was born in Fronteras, Sonora, Mexico, on July 6 or 7, 1736. He was born into a military family who originated from Basque Country of north-central Spain and south-western France at the western end of the Pyrenees Mountains on the coast of the Bay of Biscay. He enlisted in the army at the Presidio of Fronteras at the age of 16 and rose rapidly through the ranks, becoming a Captain at the age of 24 in 1761. In 1772, de Anza proposed an expedition to the Viceroy of New Spain, by land to California that was approved by the King of Spain. On January 8, 1774 de Anza led the exploration that founded the city of San Francisco, California before coming to the Ute Territory.

Governor de Anza's military authority had been granted under the 1776 Provincias Internas to provide for the governance for the Viceroyalty of New Spain (present day northern Mexico and Southwest United States). During this well documented campaign, the Spanish having turned north into South Park had lost the trail of the Comanche somewhere northwest of Pikes Peak (a mountain that appears on early Spanish maps as Sierra del Almagre). Governor de Anza knew the Comanche had been raiding other Indian tribes including the Ute and convinced them to join him in this campaign against their common enemy.

The 200 Ute were joined by 50 Jicarilla Apache. The Ute guided Governor de Anza and his military expedition of 600 hundred mounted troops north then east around Pikes Peak then down Ute Pass. This was a mountain pass the Ute knew well for they had used this trail for centuries to hunt bison in the eastern plains of Colorado between the South Platte and Arkansas Rivers. When referring to this mountain to the Spanish the Ute called it El Captain. The Spanish soldiers followed the trail used by the early French trappers and later the gold miner and pioneers who began to explore the Rocky Mountains, the Ute trails.

When Governor de Anza's military entourage caught up with the Comanche Indians, camped near the confluence of Fountain and Monument Creeks, they attacked the Indian camp causing them to take flight to the east where most of Green Horn's warriors were killed and 500 of their horses were captured. The Spanish pursued the Comanche War Chief Green Horn (Junior), along with the fleeing Comanche Indians, south and during a series of running battles fought on horseback, continuing south down Fountain Creek crossing the Arkansas River near where the city of Pueblo, Colorado stands today.

The Spanish most likely would not have been successful in pursuing and successful in stopping Green Horn Junior had it not been for the Ute Indians who guided the Spanish down Ute Pass to help them locate the Comanche camp without being detected.

Louisiana Territory and U.S. Exploration

While the Spanish were dealing with Indian problems in the West rivalry between France and England in North America was growing over possession of land west of the Appalachians. In Phil Carson's book *Across the Northern Frontier*, he writes, "By 1763 war between France and England – known in America as the French and Indian War, and in Europe as the Seven Years' War – had ended badly for France. France ceded Canada and all of Louisiana east of the Mississippi to England as a result. To Spain France ceded Louisiana west of the Mississippi." Later England's North American colonies would gain independence forming the United States. Then with the rise of Napoleon in France and his desire to restore the French Empire in North America, Napoleon forced Spain to return Louisiana to France in 1800.

In 1803, President Thomas Jefferson sent two United States representatives to meet with Napoleon to negotiate access to the Mississippi River. The Mississippi was becoming increasingly more important as a waterway for his country in its expansion to its western boundary. Napoleon, at the time, owed the U.S. $3.75 million for materials he had purchased to fund his war efforts, a considerable sum considering the entire treasury of the U.S. totaled only about $5.5 million. When President Jefferson's two representatives finally arrived in France after a month at sea aboard a wooden sailing ship, they were surprised to find that Napoleon was not interested in a long-term lease with the U.S.: he wanted to sell!

Napoleon needed funds for his war against England so the two U.S. representatives pressed ahead with the negotiations for the 828,000 square miles of France's claim to the territory of Louisiana which overnight doubled the size of the U.S. The negotiated price turned out to be less than 3 cents per acre, $11,250,000, plus the cancellation of the $3,750,000 debt owed the U.S., bringing the total purchase price to $15 million dollars.

Much of this vast newly acquired territory was relatively unknown except of course to the Native Americans who had resided in this land since at least before 10,000 B.C. They were not consulted. The purchase of the Louisiana territory opened a new era of exploration and more interaction with the Native Americans.

Thomas Jefferson appointed Clement Biddle Penrose to serve as the first commissioner of the Louisiana Territory. One of Penrose's descendants Spencer Penrose or Speck as he was called by his friends would later become a prominent leader of early Colorado Springs. To try to find out what it was they had purchased, President Jefferson sent out the Lewis and Clark Expedition, also known as the Corps of Discovery. Departing St. Louis in May of 1804 from the banks of the Mississippi River, they made their way westward over the continental divide and encountered many significant Native American tribes including the Chinook, Mandan, Lakota, Sioux and Omaha.

The first of the U.S. military explorations into the newly acquired Louisiana Territory, which included the homeland of the Ute, was led by Lt. Zebulon Montgomery Pike. Pike and his men departed into the West on July 15, 1806. His official orders were to make contact with and encourage peace between several Indian nations and to find the headwaters of the Arkansas River and the Red River. His unofficial orders may have been to spy on the strength of the Spanish military south of Arkansas River.

On November 15, 1806, Pike recorded in his journal his first sighting of a distant mountain peak that would one day bear his name, Pikes Peak or Tava as it was known to the Ute, their most sacred of all the Shining Mountains. Pike first viewed this majestic mountain from a place known as the Big Timbers; a several mile stretch of massive Cottonwood Trees growing along the Arkansas River. This location had provided shade for centuries as a meeting place for the Plains Indians to meet in council and served as a welcomed landmark for wagon trains moving westward along the Santa Fe Trail. Some of these gigantic old trees measured 26 feet in circumference. Today they are all gone; harvested for their wood by earlier settlers. The only proof they ever existed is a few pictures hanging on the wall of a museum.

History also fails to adequately mention how it was a Ute who found Lt. Pike and his men nearly starving and believing they would all perish, would lead them southward over Ute trails, out of the Shining Mountains towards the Great Sand Dunes, only to be captured by the Spanish. Pike and his men were taken to Santa Fe, then to Albuquerque and El Paso, before arriving at the Spanish Capital of Chihuahua. Ultimately Lt. Pike and his men finally made their way back to the U.S. Capital in Washington City. Zebulon Pike was eventually promoted to Brigadier General in the U.S. Army, served and was killed in action during the War of 1812.

The next significant military expedition to reach the Shining Mountains was led by Major Stephen H. Long. He and his troops followed the Platte River westward into what became the Colorado Territory. Upon first sighting the Ute's most sacred mountain Major Long directed the attention of his men southward toward what he called out as Pike's Peak, never intending it to forever become known by that name. Major Long actually would have preferred the mountain to be named James Peak in honor of one of his Lieutenants, a botanist Edwin James. Lt James was the first white man to make a recorded ascent of the Peak on July 13-15, 1820. Major Long would also have the distinction of having a Colorado mountain named in his honor, Longs Peak northwest of Denver, Colorado.

Next to explore this region was Colonel Henry Dodge leading the mighty 1st Regimental Dragoons out of Ft. Leavenworth on May 29, 1835. Known as the Dodge Expedition they first followed the South Platte River west before turning south to cross the Platte/Arkansas Divide, circling east along the edge of the Black Forest, then following the (Cherokee) trail south along Fountain Creek. Dodge and his troops then turned east, following the southern border of the United States, the Arkansas River. They paused for a few days at Old Bents Fort to refit before returning to where they began at Fort Leavenworth on September 16, 1835, a journey requiring five months. The purpose of Colonel Dodge's campaign was to impress the Native Americans with the military might of the United States, a point that may well have been lost.

Mexico had gained its independence from Spain in 1821, and the Mexican government maintained friendly relations with the Ute. But by the mid-1840s, the Ute experienced significant upheaval in their southern territory north the Santa Fe New Mexico. Mexican land grants had consumed much of the Ute territory they had depended upon for hunting for centuries to survive. As the competition for scarce resources intensified, so too did the violence in the Taos Valley and north of Espanola. In 1843, a group of Ute attacked several Mexican settlements and forced a group of farmers out of Antonito. In 1844, the Capote Ute attacked Rio Arriba settlements, likely in retaliation for a Ute who had been killed by Governor Martinez de Lejanza. The next year, the Ute attacked the settlement of Ojo Caliente.

In June of 1846, Ute chiefs met with Colonel Doniphan in Santa Fe and were induced into signing a treaty promising to remain peaceful. The Mexican-American War broke out in June of 1846, and a young thirteen year old Ute, Ouray, witnessed first-hand the military might of the U.S. Ouray, from the Tabeguache (also called Uncompahgre) band of Ute would grow to be an exceptional Ute Chief and great peacemaker. General Stephen W. Kearny and his Army of the West marched out of Leavenworth, Kansas, traveled along the Santa Fe Trail, stopping at Bent's Fort and then swooped down and captured Santa Fe on August 18, 1846. General Kearny's forces number 1,600 men, 1,500 wagons, 15,000 oxen, plus their cannons, rifles and other military equipment. Not since Governor de Anza's Comanche Campaign of 1779 had the

Ute, nor anyone else in that part of the world, seen anything to compare with the military power of the U.S.

In 1848, after Mexico had lost the Mexican-American War with the treaty of Guadalupe-Hidalgo, they ceded their land northward to the Arkansas River, which included the land the Ute controlled in what would become the northern New Mexico and southern Colorado Territories. After spending a week to set up a provisional government ensuring that northern New Mexico and the southern portion of Colorado that had not been included in the Louisiana Purchase were now effectively under control of the U.S. Government, General Kearny and most of his men pushed on to California, guided by his scout Kit Carson. To make certain the Ute remained on peaceful terms with the U.S., General Kearny sent Major William Gilpin (who would later become the first Governor of Colorado) to visit the three Southern Ute Tribes, and later that year, an unofficial treaty was arranged by Kit Carson and William Gilpin with the Mouache Ute.

The Ute recognized their traditional enemies continued to be the Cheyenne, Arapahoe, Sioux and other Native Americans, not the Mexican government or the rapidly expanding U.S. Government. The first treaty between the Ute and the U.S. Government came the following year in 1849. It was the first of many treaties, later called agreements, to contain the Ute Nation to increasingly smaller and smaller territories.

The first treaty between the U.S. Government and any Native American Indians in this west was arranged by John C. Calhoun and stipulated that the Ute would stay within their "accustomed territory"; however, it failed to specify exactly where that would be which left much to one's own interpretation. In exchange for giving up some of the land they controlled, the Ute were promised some sort of financial compensation; however, a government agent would control "their money." The Ute had to promise continuing peace and permit the U.S. to establish Indian agencies and military posts on Ute lands. The treaty was signed by Quiziachiagiate as Principle Chief of the Mouache Ute, along with 27 other Ute; however, it did not address the other six bands of the Ute Nation nor did it address peace between the Ute and other Indian tribes.

One of the Ute sub-chiefs present during these first treaty negotiations was Nevava, who historians believe was accompanied by Ouray's father and Ouray himself. Quiziachiagiate was later succeeded by Nevava who himself would later be succeeded by one of his future sub-chiefs, Ouray. The treaty provided that the Ute pledge, "their existence, as a distinct tribe, to abstain, for all time to come, from all depredations; to cease the roving and rambling habits which have hitherto marked them as a people, to confine themselves strictly to the limits which may be assigned to them; and to support themselves by their own industry, aided and directed as it may be by the wisdom, justice and humanity of the American people."

Between 1842 and 1848, another military officer, John Charles Fremont, led five expeditions into the West. Four were guided by Kit Carson; two of those cut through the San Juan Mountains, home of the South Ute bands. Fremont was very instrumental in helping America win the Mexican-American War and in 1856, was first candidate in the newly established Republican Party for President of the United States. Fremont, like Lincoln who followed him, was very much opposed to slavery. Fremont County, directly south of Pikes Peak, would become one of the seventeen original counties of the Colorado Territory and is named after John C. Fremont. Over the next several years Fremont would traverse through this area five times during his western explorations.

When Fremont first came upon the Shining Mountains, this description was captured in his report, "The whole valley is glowing and bright and all the mountain peaks are gleaming like silver." Just how much of this glowing description should be directly attributed to him or his talented wife, Jesse (Benton) Fremont, may never be known. Jesse was the daughter of Senator Thomas Hart Benton, a powerful Democrat from Missouri. She was also a very gifted writer in her own right and had political ambitions for her husband of the highest order. It is true that Abraham Lincoln can be nobly referred to as the Father of the Republican Party; however, John C. Fremont was the first Republican candidate for President of the United States.

During Fremont's return trip from California on what was his second campaign in 1843, he produced a new map of the still unmapped areas of the Great basin which he "believed to be filled with lake and rivers which have no communication with the sea..." Congress published Fremont's "Report and Map" which was used to guide thousands of immigrants overland to California and Oregon in 1845-1849, and likely encouraged the Mormons to consider Utah for settlement. Fremont and his men were crossing the Rocky Mountains by way of Middle Park, and through South Park, before they emerged along the left bank of the Arkansas River. This was very near present day Canon City, in now Fremont County, or possibly further east on or near, the Bear Basin Ranch, closer to Westcliffe, in Custer County. Here Fremont and his men witnessed a battle involving the Ute. In Fremont's word, we read:

In the evening a band of buffalo furnished a little excitement by charging through our camp. On the following day we descended the stream by an excellent buffalo trail along the open grassy bottom of the river. On our right, the Bayou was bordered by a mountainous range crested with rocky and naked peaks, and below it had a beautiful park like character of pretty, level prairies, interspersed among low spurs, wooded openly with pine and quaking asps, contrasting well with the denser pines which swept around on the mountainous sides. Descending always the valley of the stream, towards noon we descried a mounted party descending the point of a spur, and judging them to be Arapahoe – who defeated or victorious, were equally dangerous to us, and with whom a fight would be inevitable – we hurried to post ourselves as strongly as possible on some willow islands in the river. We had scarcely halted when they arrived, proving to be a party of Ute women, who told us that on the other side of the ridge their village was fighting with the Arapahoe. As soon as they had given us this information, they filled the air with cries and lamentations, which made us understand that some of their chiefs had been killed.

Extending along the river directly ahead of us as a low piney ridge, leaving between it and the stream a small open bottom on which the Ute had very injudiciously placed their village, which according to the women, numbered about three hundred warriors. Advancing in the cover of the pines, the Arapahoe, about daylight, charged into the village, driving off a great number of their horses, and killing four men, among them the principal chief of the village. They drove the horses perhaps a mile beyond the village to the end of a hollow where they had previously forted at the edge of the pines. Here the Ute had instantly attacked them in turn, and, according to the report of the women, were getting rather the best of the day. The women pressed us eagerly to join with their people, and would immediately have provided us with the best horses at the village, but it was not for us to interfere in such a conflict. Neither party were our friends or under our protection, and each was ready to prey upon us that could. But we could not but help feeling an unusual excitement at being within a few hundred yards of a fight in which five hundred men were closely engage, and hearing the sharp cracks of their rifles. We were in a bad position and subject to be attacked in it. Either party which we might meet, victorious or defeated, was certain to fall upon us, and gearing up immediately, we kept close along the pines of the ridge, having it between us and the village, and keeping the scouts on the summit to give us notice of the approach of the Indians. As we passed by the village which was immediately below us, horsemen were galloping to and fro, and groups of people were gathered around those who were wounded and dead and who were being brought in from the field.

We continued to press on, and crossing another fork which came in from the right, after having made fifteen miles from the village, fortified ourselves strongly in the pines a short distance from the river.

During the afternoon Pike's Peak had been plainly in view before us and from our encampment bore north 87° east by compass. This was a familiar object, and it had for us the face of an old friend. At its foot were the springs where we had spent a pleasant day in coming out.

Between the late 1850s and early 1860s, five major skirmishes occurred between the Ute defending their remaining hunting grounds and the Plains Indians, most especially the Arapahoe, Cheyenne and Sioux. Plains Indians had been forced from their traditional homelands further to the east by settlers moving into West, and expansion from the west eastward caught the Ute and other tribes in a pincer movement accelerated by 1848 California Gold Rush being played out and news of the 1858 Pikes Peak Gold Rush being spread. Native Americans from sea to shining sea found not only their way of life and their individual cultures being threatened, but their very existence. Nowhere was this tragic clash of cultures more violently felt then at the heart of the Ute Nation in the Shining Mountains.

While traveling through South Park in 1852, Kit Carson and his foster-son, Will Drannan, witnessed a furious battle between the Ute and the Comanche fought along the creek east of Fortification Hill (present day Florissant, CO). On March 30, 1852, Commander Sumner assigned Maj. George A.H. Blake to lead the First Dragoons and H Company, Third Infantry, to establish the first fort among the Ute. It was located in the foothills below Mount Blanca and it was built of logs placed vertically on end with mud chinked between the logs and required the work of 150 men. It was named Fort Massachusetts and was relocate at the site of the present day Fort Garland, Colorado. The Fort has been reconstructed to resemble what a portion of the fort would have looked like at the time when Kit Carson served as its Commanding Officer where he greeted many Ute on the floor of his living room.

On December 25, 1854 Mouache Ute, led by Chief Blanco, attacked Fort Pueblo leaving fifteen males dead (including soldiers, traders and local Mexican farmers). The Ute warriors abducted one woman and two small boys during several previous raids they had conducted across the San Luis Valley. Some historians contend that these raids may have been in retaliation for what was believed to have been the deliberate act of annihilation when the Ute men were given blanket coats by the military infected with smallpox. Other historians state that if items were given to the Ute with smallpox it was inadvertently done. Many Mouache men, including most of their leaders, had died when the smallpox epidemic broke out on their way to their traditional hunting grounds.

Leaving Taos in early March 1855, Kit Carson served as a guide under Colonel T.T. Fauntleroy for his 500 soldiers attached to four companies of volunteers under Colonel Ceran St. Vrain. This campaign consisted of seven battles to suppress Chief Blanco and his Southern Ute Warriors. This campaign culminated on March 19, 1855, near Saguache where 40 Ute warriors were killed in battle. Ouray would have been twenty-two years of age at the time. This battle which may have been Ouray's first official act as an Uncompahgre Ute Chief, occurred during one of the last battles in August 1855. Chief Ouray asked Shavano, one of Ouray's most loyal friends and trusted warriors, to send runners to warn Kit Carson of an impending attack from Ute Chief Kaneache.

Ouray and Shavano later rode to where Kit Carson was camped near Raton Pass, picking up twenty Ute warriors along the way and helped defend the US Military against the attack from Chief Kaneache and his Ute Warriors. Six Ute were killed during the fighting and Chief Kaneache was wounded during the fighting and taken prisoner. After losing the seventh consecutive fight with the US Military the Ute again asked for peace with the white man this time in September of 1855. Ouray believed many more Ute would be killed following Chief Kaneache's leadership and believed further fighting would only amount to the death of more Ute warriors. Kit Carson could speak Ute fluently and had become trusted for being a man of his word. The bond between Ouray and Kit Carson was one that would endure throughout their lives.

Although Chief Kaneache was later released after his wounds had healed, he harbored severe resentment against Ouray all the rest of his days.

In the late summer of 1856, thirty-eight Arapahoe and Cheyenne Indians stole about forty Ute horses. Chief Nevava assembled ten Ute warriors, including Ouray, Shavano and Colorow, then rode out in pursuit intent on recovering their stolen horses. Chief Nevava had planned to confront the superior number of enemy warriors head-on; however when they caught up to their horses still in the possession of their enemies, Ouray persuaded Nevava to ambush them rather than a direct assault. The Ute killed eight enemy warriors and recovered all of their stolen horses without losing a single Ute warrior. This outcome dramatically elevated Ouray's leadership and skill as a warrior in the eyes of the other Ute, most especially those who knew the outcome would have been different had Ouray not intervened to suggest a better battle plan.

In 1858, a large band of Cheyenne and Arapahoe had a day long battle with the Ute around Monument Park, six or eight miles north of Colorado Springs. In each of the major skirmishes between the Ute and their Native American adversaries, Ouray distinguished himself as a fierce warrior among the Tabeguache.

With but a few notable exceptions, Fort El Pueblo, Christmas Day 1854, the Battle of the Little Big Horn in 1876, and Battle of Milk Creek in 1879, the Ute almost always remained friendly with the white man and often rode alongside them in battle. Literally from A-Z, from Anza (Governor de Anza 1779) to Zebulon (Lieutenant Pike 1806) and seemingly nearly anywhere Col. Kit Carson rode into harm's way the Ute rode alongside him. At the Battle of Adobe Walls, November 1863, Kit Carson's 400 cavalry and a handful of scouts were attacked by 1500 plains Indians. When things looked bleak, Kit Carson pulled the two Ute aside to let them know they did not need to die there and were free to go. The two Ute chose to stay and fight alongside of Kit Carson.

Kit Carson was once offered his choice for an opportunity to command either two hundred regular U.S. cavalry into battle or fifty Ute warriors. He chose the fifty Ute. Christopher "Kit" Carson was close friends with Chief Ouray and served as the Ute Indian Agent in the Colorado Territory from 1853, until he tendered his resignation in 1859 to join the Union Army at the onset of the American Civil War.

In Irving Howbert's book *Indians of the Pike's Peak Region,* he documents another battle pitting the Ute against the Cheyenne, Arapahoes and the Sioux in 1859 fought "...six miles north of Colorado City, in the valley now occupied by the Modern Woodmen's Home. There were several hundred warriors on each side and the battle was of unusual duration, continuing for almost an entire day. The Ute were finally victorious and drove their enemies back to the plains."

Irving Howbert, arrived in Colorado City in 1861 with his father, the Reverend Howbert, who built the first Methodist Church, further describes in his book, *Indians of the Pike's Peak Region*, "Until 1864, every spring after the white settlers came into this region, war-parties of Cheyenne, Arapahoes, and Sioux would come trailing in from the plains, pass through Colorado City, stopping long enough to beg food from the families living near the line of their march and then go on to the soda springs; here they would tarry long enough to make an offering to the Great Spirit who was supposed to be manifest in the bubbling waters, and then follow, in single file, up the Ute Pass into the South Park, where they would scout around until they had found a band of Ute. If they succeeded in surprising the latter, they would probably come back with a lot of extra ponies and sometimes with captured squaws and children, in which case they would exhibit a jubilant air; but at other times on their return, they would present such a dejected appearance that one could readily surmise that they had suffered defeat. These annual visits were discontinued after the tribes became involved in warfare with the whites."

During the late 1850s and early 1860s many pioneers came to Ute territory in search for gold, still further encroaching land used by the Ute. Various failed attempts to create a settlement near the base of Pikes Peak failed. Then in 1859 a group of businessmen decided the confluence of Fountain and Camp Creeks at the base of the Ute Pass was a good location. Colorado City was founded, August of 1859, as a gold mining supply town. The city founders intended to use the old Ute Indian trail to freight materials coming from the east across the Santa Fe Trail, west up the Ute Pass to supply the gold fields located west of Pikes Peak. Miners were following Ute Pass up the side of Pikes Peak to the gold fields of South Park stopping in Colorado City. Old Colorado City grew to about 300 residents by 1860 while it was still part of the Kansas Territory. The other main mountain corridor leading from Denver to South Park (U.S. Highway 285) was established over Kenosha Pass. Kenosh is the Ute word for their urn shaped pitch covered water basket-bottles which held anywhere from 3 quarts to 2 1/2 gallons of water. The Ute often camped near Fountain Creek near Colorado City.

New settlements occurred all over what became early El Paso County. Fountain was founded in 1859. Colorado Springs was founded in 1871 followed by Manitou in 1872. Monument was incorporated in 1879. In the 1880s the town of Cascade was the first town heading up Ute Pass followed by other towns along the Midland Railway. These first settlements were in the Kansas Territory. Later settlements, after 1861, would be in the new Colorado Territory. Finally Colorado would acquire Statehood in 1876.

The discovery of gold in Colorado and the amount of settlers coming into the Ute territories would bring changes to the Ute Nation. Ouray and Kit Carson's friendships grew to where they became very close personal friends. This friendship was aided by the fact they each could speak Ute, Spanish as well as English and they each demonstrated a sincere respect for one another's diverse cultures. Kit Carson often spoke to Ouray about the importance of establishing a written treaty that better recognized the boundaries of the Ute Nation in order to maintain peaceful relationship with the white miners who came for gold, then stayed on to establish farms. Ouray knew his friend spoke the truth and struggled to find a way for the Ute to remain in the Shining Mountains, a place that was rapidly filling up with white men in search of the yellow metal. Ouray finally decided to consult Chief Nevava about his and Kit Carson's concerns hoping to find a peaceful solution or a compromise.

When Ouray approached Chief Nevava about this need to establish their territorial boundaries as Kit Carson had suggested, Nevava readily dismissed the notion because everyone knew where the Ute Territories *"had been forever"* and the Ute could always defend their mountain passes, with stones and sticks if necessary. Ouray persisted until Chief Nevava finally consented to at least allow Ouray to go into the Pikes Peak area to see what the white man was up to and report back.

The Ute could not understand white man's concept of owning or possessing the land. They simply could not comprehend how any man could own the land around them any more than how a man could claim to own the air around them, given by the Creator to everyone, for all the People to breathe. The Ute did not believe this land where the Creator had brought them to live at the very beginning of time, here in the Shining Mountains, even belonged to them. Quite the reverse, in fact, is true; the Ute belong to the land.

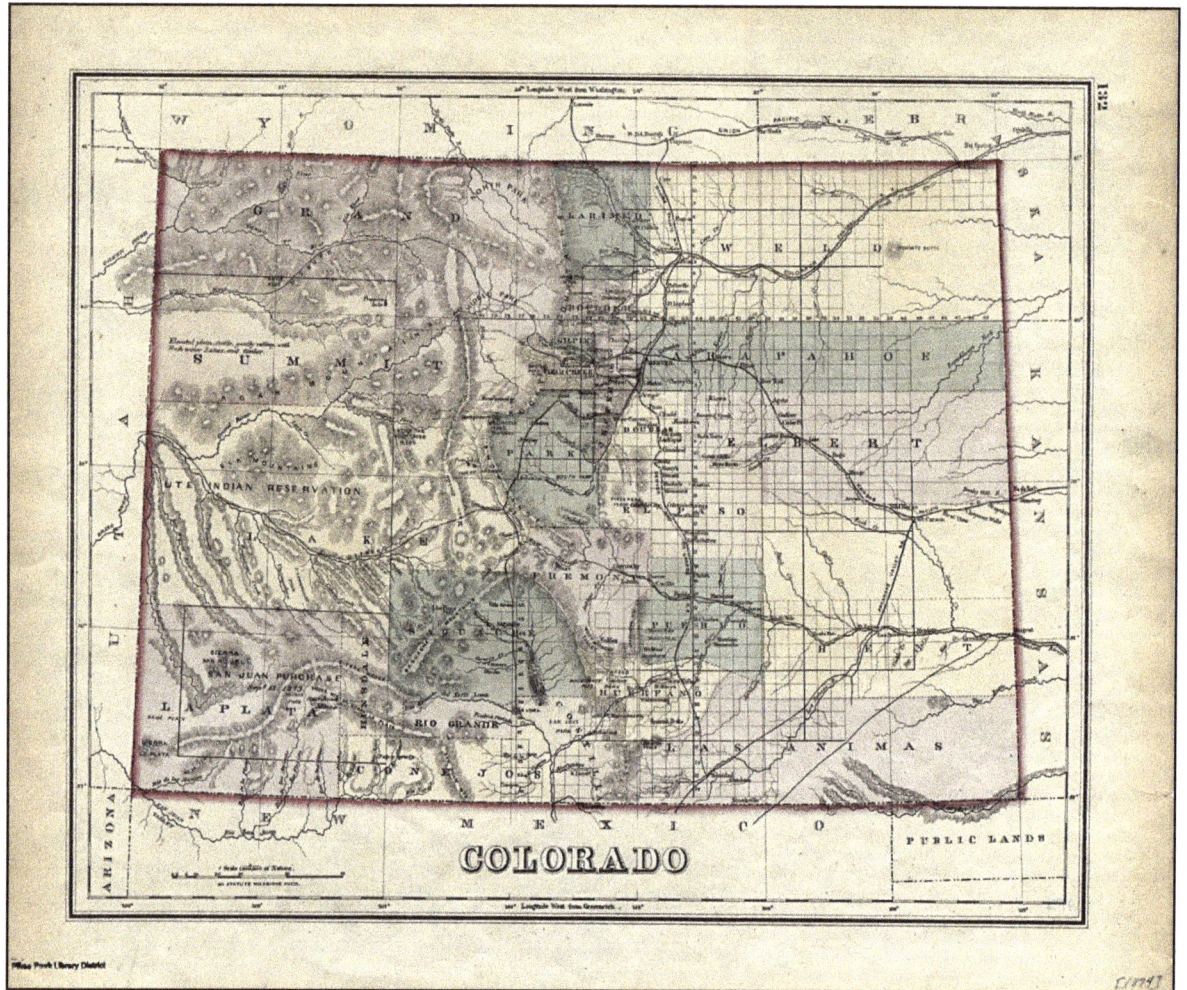

1874 Colorado Territory Map: This is a map of the Colorado Territory as it existed two years before Colorado became as state. Bordering El Paso County to the east was the Indian Reserve for the Cheyenne and Arapahoe Tribes. This Indian Reservation had also appeared on earlier maps of the Nebraska and Kansas Territories (1855) and extended east to the Kansas state line. By 1874 this Reservation no longer existed, a consequence of the 1864 and 1868 Indian Wars. The Ute Indian Reservation is shown extending west from the Continental Divide to the Utah state line. Also depicted is the adjoining land to the south acquired from the Ute for mining purposes in what was commonly known as the San Juan Purchase (Sept 13, 1873). This map is from the Special Collections of the Pikes Peak Library District (PPLD) and is reprinted with permission of the PPLD.

Chapter 7 - El Paso County, Colorado Territory (1861-Present Day)
Never underestimate the power of storytelling,
it teaches how one should strive to live.

The legislation that established the Colorado Territory was signed by President James Buchanan on February 28, 1861. This act may have been his last official duty as President of the United States. The signing took place unceremoniously in the White House as President Buchanan paused from packing his personal belongings long enough to sign the executive order. President Buchanan was moving out of the White House to make room for the incoming U.S. President Abraham Lincoln. Lincoln appointed William Gilpin of Missouri to serve as the first Governor of the Colorado Territory. El Paso County became one of the 17 original counties established by the Colorado Legislature on November 1, 1861. Governor Gilpin appointed a three-man committee to select El Paso County's first three County Commissioners.

There had been two previous failed attempts to establish this new Territory but with tensions mounting between the north and the south the legislation was rushed through. The rumblings of the Civil War looming just over the horizon was the catalyst to establish the new Territory where gold had been discovered in the Pikes Peak Region. One of the stumbling blocks had ironically been the proposed name for what was to have been the Jefferson Territory intended to honor the third President of the United States Thomas Jefferson. Opponents to the proposed name expressed concerns there may be confusion that the Territory was being named after the Senator from Mississippi, Jefferson Davis, thereby giving the appearance the Territory would be aligned with the southern cause.

At the last hour the proponents of the legislation glanced briefly at a map of the proposed Jefferson Territory (JT) and saw the name of a small town near the center of the map, Colorado City. They quickly changed the proposed name of the new territory to Colorado and the legislation passed. There were several other reasonable names that were considered; including Cibola, El Dorado and Idaho. Then there were other names that were not quite as reasonable; including Lulu and Bill Williams. Bill Williams was a frontiersman who was widely recognized throughout the Rocky Mountains. He had been hired by Colonel John Fremont to lead his fifth expedition to chart a new route to the west coast of California.

The job of scouting for Fremont's fourth expedition had first been offered to Kit Carson, the famous scout who had led Colonel Fremont's previous three campaigns. Kit Carson turned down the offer as Fremont was insistent the campaign had to start out immediately, even though it was in the middle of winter. Carson knew the trip across these rugged mountain peaks at this time of year could only end in disaster, which it did costing the lives of several of Fremont's men. Bill Williams did not survive this failed attempt to cross the Ute's Shining Mountains. Fremont convalesced in Carson's home in Taos after being rescued. Bill Williams had been well known among the Ute, having been married to eight different Ute women throughout his lifetime.

Two major 19th Century historic events that helped shape the American West brought about irrevocable and dramatic change in the life the Ute Nation. First, the acquisition of the Louisiana Purchase from France in 1803 provided legal title to this land in the American West, at least in the eyes of the U.S. Citizen. Native Americans would not be recognized as citizens by the U.S. government until 1924. Second, The Pikes Peak Gold Rush of 1858-61 provided the financial incentive to pursue those dreams, bringing settlement into land once occupied by the Ute Nation.

The story of the founding of the Colorado Territory and thus the establishment for the foundation upon which the State of Colorado would someday be built, can be told through the story of two dissimilar groups of adventurous rugged people with one distinct element of similarity; the color of gold. These two groups were known as the Greene Russell Party and the Lawrence Party. The Greene Russell Party consisted of about 75 men from Georgia; most were related to one another or affiliated to the Cherokee Nation. They were experienced hard rock miners who passed through the Rocky Mountains on their way to California. Later they would return to what became the Colorado Territory to mine for gold.

The Lawrence Party was a group of hard working businessmen from eastern Kansas who principally came to mine gold from the gold miners. One lesson learned from the California Gold Strike was that there was more money to be made by supplying the gold miners, than in mining itself. This was a lesson a man like Levi Strauss took to heart and made his fortune selling reinforced jeans to the miners. Over the next century Levi's jeans would become the world's bestselling article of clothing. Another iconic symbol of the American West is the famous Stetson cowboy hat, established by John B. Stetson in 1865. While riding through the mining camps around Pikes Peak, John Stetson discovered the miners needed a sturdy hat which would maintain its shape with a wide brim to shield the back of their necks from the sun while they bent over streams panning for gold day after day.

When the California Gold Strike played out in 1858, Greene Russell and his party of Forty-Niners were returning from California and upon reaching the place where they had camped ten years earlier along the Cherokee Trail at the confluence of Cherry Creek and the South Platte, they discovered gold. Most of the Greene Russell party stayed to continue panning for gold and began a search further upstream to find the source of this gold somewhere up high in the mountains to the west. A few of the Greene Russell party took their gold and headed directly east following what became known as the Smoky Hill Trail arriving in Lawrence, Kansas where word of their Pikes Peak gold strike spread throughout the world. The people who decided to head west to find their fortune in gold the following spring of 1859 became known as the Fifty-Niners. These two groups, miners searching for gold and businessmen desiring to make money from the mining industry, along with the ever growing numbers of immigrants who were looking for new opportunities for their families would back the push for statehood.

Indian Wars and Ute Peacemakers

The biggest threat the settlers of El Paso County and other surrounding counties in the Colorado Territory had was the same threat the Ute encountered, other Native American Tribes. In 1862, Indian Agent William Arny reported 400 Plains Indians had attacked twelve Ute, nine of whom were either killed or gravely wounded, the last three fought off the attack. These plains Indians, believed to have been from the Cheyenne and Arapahoe Tribes, finally gave up the battle having suffered far too many losses to justify trying to finish off the remaining three Ute.

Referring again to Irving Howbert exceptional book *Indians of the Pikes Peak Region,* in regarding the Indian Troubles of 1864 he provides us a rare glimpse back to the spring of 1864 by someone who was actually there at the time. Howbert wrote the following:

> As I have before mentioned war parties of Cheyenne and Arapahoe continued to make occasional trips through the Ute Pass to the mountain in search of their enemies, the Ute, until 1864. As these war parties seldom tarried long in this vicinity, their presence was not seriously objected to during the first two or three years, but after rumors of impending trouble with them became current, their visits were looked upon with a good deal of apprehension.

> Early in 1863, they began to attack and rob wagon trains, steal horses, and threaten exposed settlements, but nothing occurred to cause any great alarm in the immediate Pike's Peak region, until the spring of 1864. During a very considerable portion of the next four years; however, the people of El Paso County experienced all the horrors of Indian warfare. ...At the time hostilities began, I was little more than eighteen years old...About the 20th of June, 1864, word reached Colorado City that a day or two previously, the Hungate family, living on Running Creek about forty miles northeast of Colorado City, had been murdered by Indians.

> The father and mother had been shot down and mutilated with horrible brutality, and the children who had tried to escape had been pursued and killed, so that not one of the family was left alive. This news made the people of Colorado City and the settlers along Fountain and on the Divide, very uneasy, and of course, after that, they were constantly on the lookout, not knowing where the savages might next appear. ...Two or three weeks after the murder of the Hungate family, some cattle herders came into Colorado City late one evening and told of having seen near Austin's Bluff, a half a dozen mounted Indians who seemed to be acting mysteriously...Early the following morning an armed party went to the place where the Indians had been seen, found their trail, and followed it.

In this way it was discovered that, sometime during the previous night, the Indians had been on the hill that overlooks Colorado City on the north, and that the trail from that point led into the mountains. ... At that time I was living with my father on the west side of Camp Creek, about half-way between Colorado City and the Garden of the Gods... While I was helping to drive them (Howbert family's cattle) into the corral adjacent to our house, I happened to look up the valley of Camp Creek, and there, about three-quarters of a mile away, I saw six mounted Indians leading an extra horse. They were going easterly along the old Indian trail, which...ran just south of the Garden of the Gods.

Howbert goes on to describe in considerable detail about helping to organize a posse of men from Colorado City who overcame these six Indians later that same evening camped along Fountain Creek, just north of where the Colorado College soccer field sits today. He continues to write, "We knew the tribes to which these Indians belonged were at war with the whites, and that, unless they were on their way to fight the Ute, they were here on no peaceable errand so far as our people were concerned. Their course in going only to the foot of the mountains showed that they were not seeking the Ute, and their actions...proved conclusively that they were here as scouts of a larger party..."

While attempting to take the six Indians into custody, and escort them to Colorado City, the six mounted Indians were fired upon in the dark and only one rode away apparently unharmed. Being too dark to continue, Howbert described how he and the other posse members returned to Colorado City, but the following morning returned to where the "mêlée" had occurred to discover, "marks upon the ground showing where the dead and wounded had evidently lain. Several years afterward, we learned from the Cheyenne that three of this scouting party had been killed outright, one was so seriously wounded that he died shortly thereafter, another was slightly wounded, and one had escaped unhurt. The last, with the aid of the one slightly wounded, had carried off and buried the dead during the night."

Later that summer, in 1864, two hundred Ute Indians were camped at the head of Monument Creek where Palmer Lake is now located when six or seven Arapahoe Indians sneaked up on them and stole twenty ponies. About thirty Ute pursued them fifty miles south along Fountain Creek and caught up with them where the Arapahoe braves had finally stopped under the shade of a cottonwood grove to rest (believed to be about twenty miles north of where Pueblo is today). The Arapahoe, believing they were far enough away from the Ute, had fallen fast asleep and, as was the common among many Native Indian tribes, did not post sentries. When the raiding Arapahoe braves were overtaken by the Ute, they were all killed and their scalps had been taken. The stolen Ute ponies then were rounded up and the Ute returned to their camp known today as Monument Creek at the foot of Pikes Peak.

Fear was growing with the settlers regarding the fearsome Dog Soldiers. Dog Soldiers were a group of warriors made up from mixed tribes, Cheyenne and Lakota, whose goal was to fight the white man to the death. The Dog Soldiers were angry at chiefs that had signed treaties that took away land and placed constraints upon them by the United States. The Dog Soldiers had participated in several atrocities across the Colorado Territory. The Ute had refused to join the Dog Soldiers.

By the end of 1864, settlers were calling for something to be done regarding the problems with the Indians. John Milton Chivington, considered a hero by some for destroying the southern supplies ending a Civil War Battle at Glorieta Pass in today's New Mexico, would be called Bloody Butcher by others for his leadership role in the Battle at Sand Creek. Chivington, on the morning of November 29, 1864, ordered his 700 troops to attack the Indian village in what became known as the Sand Creek Massacre. Much debate still occurs among historians regarding the number that died in this battle, the necessity of the battle and atrocities that occurred during and after the battle. For the purposes of this book, we look at the battle in the light of the total picture of Indian and American relationships and how it would play a part in the removal of Indians to reservations.

It is interesting to note that Irving Howbert later wrote a first-hand account of this battle in which he participated in as an enlisted man at eighteen years of age. Howbert would become a well respected leader in Colorado Springs and in his autobiography he would defend Chivington claiming that there were a number of warriors at the battle, a number equal to the number of Volunteers. He said that due to the Colorado Volunteers having rounded up the Indians horses earlier, the Indians were at a disadvantage having to fight on foot. Howbert believed the attack was retaliation for attacks on settlers in Colorado and for the torture and killing of American citizens in the three previous years. He said that many scalps from white people, including women and children were confiscated after the attack. Howbert felt that false testimony was given against Chivington by Samuel F. Tappan due to military rivalry.

At the conclusion of Irving Howbert's book, *Indians of the Pikes Peak Region*, he describes the murders of at least a dozen El Paso County citizens, at the hands of, "…the Sioux, Cheyenne, and Arapahoe, the most crafty and bloodthirsty savages upon the American continent." These victims of the Indian Wars included Charlie Everhart, the Robbins boys (George 8, Franklin 11), Edward Davis, Job Talbert, six year old Leona Johnson and Jonathan Lincoln. Jonathan Lincoln was unarmed and knelling on his knees when he was killed just north of the El Paso County line in Spring Valley along Cherry Creek.

Irving Howbert, who lived and fought through these four years of Indian attacks, summarized his feelings at the end of his final chapter, concluding, "…it now seems a wonder that we were not wiped off the face of the earth…the reason that we were not exterminated was the fact of our contiguity to the country of their hereditary enemies, the Ute, for whom, on account of their fighting ability, they had a wholesome respect."

Clearly there were atrocities on both sides. Many felt Sand Creek was justified due to the loss of life the Indians had taken upon settlers. Many felt it was beyond justification for Chivington's men to mutilate the dead after the battle was over or even for the battle have occurred at all. It seems to be easier for us today to understand the resentment of the Native Americans to the treatment they were given by the U.S. Government, than to understand the fear felt by the settlers due to Indian attacks that took property and lives of their families and neighbors.

In 1865-66, a large body of Ute camped peacefully for several months along the bank of Fountain Creek near Colorado City. During the winter of 1866-67, a thousand or more of the same tribe camped between Balanced Rock and Boiling Springs.

In the late summer of 1866, Ute Chief Ouray, his wife Chipeta, and enough Tabeguache Ute families to make up about 100 lodges set up camp on Mosca Pass. While there a rebellious Mouache Ute Chief, named Kaniache and several members of his band had stolen some horses and corn near present-day Trinidad, soliciting a response from the Third Calvary out of Ft. Stevens. When word of this reached Chief Ouray, he immediately rode south to tell Kit Carson, the Commander of Ft. Garland, who was responsible for these raids.

As more and more settlers arrived, tension among Native American tribes competing for resources that were shrinking and tension between settlers and Native Americans would grow. The story of how these tensions would affect the Ute can perhaps be told through the lives of the two most well-known of the Ute Indians, Chief Ouray (1833-1880) and his wife Chipeta (1843-1924) who both learned to speak English. Chief Ouray's mother, was a Tabeguache Ute, and his father was a Jicarilla Apache (Jicarilla means little basket) who became a Tabeguache Ute after marrying Ouray's mother which was a common practice among many Indian tribes. Chief Ouray's Indian name may have been "Arrow" although there remains some discrepancy regarding this point, and even the spelling of Ouray is not consistent in the early historical record.

Chipeta's early life is also somewhat unclear; however, the most accepted account of her early childhood recounts a story of a Ute hunting party approaching a small circle of Kiowa-Apache tepees in the shade of a cottonwood grove. There were small columns of smoke coming from the camp, but no horses or movement of any kind could be seen. The men also noticed there was no noise of any kind, not even the usual barking of dogs who always alerted an Indian camp of a stranger's approach. As the Ute hunting party walked cautiously through the small cluster of silent tepees, they began finding dead bodies of men, women and children many of whom died with weapons clutched in their hands, obviously attempting to defend themselves from a sudden and violent attack.

As the Ute hunters quietly backed out of this place of death, the silence was broken by the sound of a child's wail. One Ute brave made his way back into the camp to discover a two-year-old toddler crying among the dead bodies, no doubt her family. The Ute man picked the child up and held her gently in his arms to comfort her, the sole survivor of a massacre. He took the child home to his Ute family, and she was adopted into his Tabeguache band. Her new family gave her the Ute name Chipeta meaning White Singing Bird. She grew to become known to be a hard worker with a melodious laugh and a beautiful singing voice and later taught herself to play the guitar.

Chipeta was Ouray's second wife, his first died shortly after their son Paron was born. Chipeta was a devoted wife and step mother to Paron, but tragically, while on his first bison hunt with Ouray, Paron was abducted by the Arapahoe. Paron was five at the time and Ouray would spend much of his remaining years continuing to search for his only son.

By 1860, at the age of 27, Ouray had risen to become a sub-chief under Chief Nevava, to whom he was very loyal. Ouray became widely recognized as a very capable enforcer for Chief Nevava, killing those who opposed Chief Nevava. Some factors that led Ouray to become a component of peace between the United States and the Ute were his first-hand experience in seeing the might of the U.S. military, his friendship with Kit Carson and his knowledge of the English language and his desire to stop the bloodshed that was claiming the lives of the Ute.

Chief Ouray led the first Ute Indian peace delegation to Washington City (DC) in April 1863 during the Indian conflicts. There he met with President Abraham Lincoln who presented Chief Ouray with an ebony cane along with the Lincoln Peace Medal often seen in later photos of Chief Ouray and Chipeta. After the Civil War had ended, Chief Ouray led another Ute Delegation back to Washington City to meet with President Ulysses S. Grant in January, 1872. The following year, Ouray returned to the nation's capital with another Ute delegation and met once again with President Grant on October 24th, 1873. This time the Ute Chief knew they would have to concede their claim to the San Juan Mountains rich in silver.

On June 25th 1876, General George Armstrong Custer and his 7th Calvary were wiped out by Indians during the Battle of the Little Big Horn in Montana. The only known survivor, at the time, was Custer's horse Comanche. The warring Indians were primarily comprised of Cheyenne and Sioux warriors; however, two Ute were there at the time the fighting broke out. One of the Ute was a warrior, known by the name Yellow Nose. He was there visiting his sister who had married into the Cheyenne tribe. Yellow Nose rode into the battle on horseback once the fighting broke out. According to Ute elders, it was Yellow Nose who killed Custer. He was said to have snatched a guidon from the field of battle and rode down on Custer, who had earlier dismounted, and drove the staff through Custer's chest.

Between the years 1850 and 1890, there were approximately 1,400 "fights" involving Native

Americans with soldiers or civilians. The Indian Wars, along with fighting between Indian tribes that involved the Ute, would profoundly impact the Ute, for these bloody conflicts soon restricted their safe passage to their sacred trees and ancestral bison hunting grounds on the grassy plains east of the Shining Mountains.

Efforts to confine the Ute to reservations came to a tragic head in 1879. The Ute agent Nathan Meeker that was assigned to the White River Ute was adamant that the Ute build homes, settle down and become agricultural. In an effort to reach this end he began to plow a meadow the Ute use to graze their horses and where they had a race track. The White River Ute warned him not to plow and in an argument, Meeker was pushed down. He called for troops and the Ute felt that no good could come if the troops came on the reservation. They felt that the troops being brought in was an act of war. The Ute attacked at Milk Creek, September 29 through October 5, 1879 in what became known as the Meeker Massacre. At the Agency, Meeker and his staff were killed. Major Thornburgh was killed and his troops surrounded. This would become the leverage needed to force remaining Ute in Colorado onto reservations.

The various Ute tribes all stood together in support of the White River Ute. In January a small group of Ute would make a trip to Washington D.C. to discuss their fate with the Bureau of Indian Affairs. This would be Chief Ouray's last trip to Washington D.C. He was joined by Chipeta. As was the custom of most delegations visiting the Nation's Capital, Ouray and Chipeta, along with most of the Ute delegation, had their photos taken by famous photographer Matthew W. Brady at his studio located at 627 Pennsylvania Avenue, NW. Ouray died on August 24, 1880. The Ute were the last Native Americans in the State of Colorado to be forced onto reservations, a direct result of the 1879 Battle at Milk Creek, known more widely as the Meeker Massacre, depending of course upon which side of Milk Creek one stands.

Descendants of the seven Ute tribes, the people who cultivated the Ute Prayer Trees in the Pikes Peak Region, were forced onto Reservations pursuant to the 1880 Ute Agreement. The Ute still live today on what are legally defined as a Native Sovereign Nation (NSN), situated in the far southwest part of the state where four states; Utah, New Mexico, Arizona and Colorado converge, an area known as the Four Corners. The Southern Ute Reservation is located south of Durango and adjoining it to the west is the Ute Mountain Ute Reservation, today surrounded on three sides by one of the best preserved ancient Native American Indian ruins, known as Mesa Verde. The Northern Ute Tribe is located on the Uintah-Ouray Reservation headquartered near Ft. Duchesne, Utah.

In 1890, the Commissioner of Indian Affairs, Thomas J. Morgan, directed that all Native American Indians who were to receive any allotments must adopt the white man's custom of using family names. He prohibited the translation of Indian names to English, finding many to be too difficult for the white man to pronounce, but did allow Indian names to be shortened where they could be recognizable. He also authorized the use of a Christian given name to precede the Indian name as the surname. This plan was later revived and enforced by President Theodore Roosevelt in 1902 and explains how many Ute, including Dr. James Jefferson, came to have the first and last names of a white man.

The U.S. Government enacted another law in 1890 which would affect not people, but places. The United States Board on Geographic Names directed the discontinued use of the possessive apostrophe on all federal maps and signs so as not to show ownership of the place. Tava, Pike's Peak, would become known as Pikes Peak. On June 3, 1905, President Teddy Roosevelt signed the Presidential order that created the San Juan National Forest which includes the Weminuche Wilderness, once the winter home of many Ute bands.

From the turn of the century until today, the Ute remain a deeply spiritual and resilient people that embrace their culture and are rightly proud of their history. At the time the Ute were put on reservations, there was a desire to "civilize" them, which meant they were to live as the white man lived (in houses, dressing like white man, going to white schools and giving each individual man an allotment of land). This did not work well with the Ute who were used to living as a tribe. Some Elders pushed for programs that would make the Ute take part in the culture they were being forced to join while others were against becoming like white man.

Instead of farming, which many Ute did not like, and was not really possible because much of the land they were assigned to was too arid, many Ute took to raising sheep. Assimilation into American culture had many challenges. Cultural difference between Ute and the rest of America caused poverty and unemployment. Many Ute that left the reservation to go to college or find employment did not return except to visit. For the early years on the reservation, many adult Ute can tell personal accounts of prejudice and racism.

Today the Ute people have three reservations with their own tribal government. They still practice tribal customs such as the Bear Dance and the Sun Dance and take pride in their culture. They have also developed industries such as tourism, agriculture, mining, natural gas and gaming. Leadership within each tribe works toward the health and welfare of the Ute. Today much effort is being made to keep the customs and culture of the Ute alive for future generations. The Ute still know Pikes Peak as Tava, the Sun Mountain, which remains laced with ancient Ute trails accented by their sacred Ute Indian Prayer Trees.

Abert Trailmarker Tree: This massive old Trailmarker Tree is located on private property midway up the right bank of a tributary to Black Squirrel Creek, in the Black Forest east of Highway 83, in El Paso County, Colorado. This Culturally Modified Tree displays the classic single 30° bend of the trunk, the oval shape of the large trunk supporting the weight of the tree above bend, and clear evidence of ligature tie-down marks. The tree also displays the classic primary trunk, which resembles a branch, extending to the upper left in this photo above the bend. This original trunk is a perfect example of the diameter of the tree as well as the possible height of the tree at the time it was tied or staked down. The full orange color of the bark suggests the age of this tree to be about 400 years old. The direction the tree is pointing, southeast is most intriguing. This Trailmarker is pointing downstream where several other UPTs are located. Several of these CMTs are the classic variety of Ute Burial Trees, but what is somewhat of a mystery are 3-4 large mounds which appear to be man made; the Ute did not traditionally build mounds. Above the bank behind this tree to the west is a lush grassy meadow with an amazing view of Tava (Pikes Peak).

Trailmarker USAFA: This intriguing old UPT is located on the U.S. Air Force Academy property, in Colorado Springs, Colorado. It can be found on the east side of Stadium Blvd, directly north and across the road to the east of the USAFA Football stadium. The tree is visible from the east curb looking northeast approximately 300 yards across a dry creek bed. This Trailmarker Tree stands on the left bank and has definite ligature marks around the bark at the inside of the bend. It can be distinguished by two primary extending trunks which point in a northeasterly direction towards Monument Creek near the confluence of Black Squirrel Creek and may even be pointing towards the Cherokee Trail. The Cherokee were known to have traveled across a vast trail system which extended from the Atlantic to the Pacific Oceans. The Cherokee Trail in Colorado connected the Santa Fe Trail, which ran along the left bank of the Arkansas River, north through the Black Forest, then connected to the Oregon Trail crossing the South Platte River near Denver before turning westward. Several Cherokee associated with the Green Russell Party were partially responsible for the discovery of gold in the Pikes Peak Region which led to the establishment of the Colorado Territory (CT) in 1861. This tree does have some peeled bark, primarily to the root area, which may be human caused; however the author is cautious when examining peeled bark especially at ground level as there could be other contributing natural and/or man made factors. There is a remarkable split in the bark, visible in this photo, with two unusual branches extending outward from this split in the bark and a third on the opposite side of this trunk extending outward to the northeast. The Cherokee used Trailmarker Trees extensively for marking trails including those that pointed towards water, as did the Ute, but what is rather unusual about these lower branches is they appear that they may have been grafted. The Cherokee did have a written language and were known to have developed the skill required to graft branches and transplant trees. It is believed this tree was used as a Trailmarker or possibly a Message Tree and may have pointed towards water. There are other Ute Prayer Trees in the immediate vicinity; however there was extensive construction and landscaping in this area during the 1950-1960's when the US Air Force Academy was being built. Attributing every CMT in the Pikes Peak Region exclusively to the Ute may not be historically accurate, especially when a CMT is found that may be slightly out of the norm in a vicinity where other tribal nations where believed to have traveled. This CMT is very old and clearly predates the founding of the USAFA; perhaps even by 150+ years.

Dancing Coyote Canyon: This old CMT is located on the land now owned by Dancing Coyote Canyon, northwest of the Eleven Mile Reservoir, in Park County, Colorado. The tree has definite evidence of peeled bark, as shown in the photo, a slight human caused distortion of the trunk, along with an area opposite the peeled bark where pine pitch was most likely harvested. The peeled bark pattern does not appear consistent with the ceremonial bark removal pattern found on many trees in El Paso, Teller and Eagle Counties, which may suggest it was extracted for non-ceremonial or utilitarian or perhaps nutritional purposes or was peeled by someone who may have been Ute but not a Medicine Man. This peeled bark pattern does not follow the typical tree blaze patterns used by the white man for simply marking a trail. What gives further credibility to the likelihood of this being a Ute Prayer Tree is the fact it was found in close association with other Ute artifacts, including the Ute rock water basins.

Trailmarker Tree Teller County: This sacred Ute Trailmarker Tree is located on the Clark Ranch in Teller County, Colorado. The Clark Ranch is located 23 miles west of Colorado Springs on Highway 24 between the towns of Woodland Park and Divide. This historic 855-acre ranch was first settled in the 1860's near a small thermal artesian spring. The original settlers found what the Ute knew all along, that they and their livestock would find water flowing year round from the spring. The first cabin built on the ranch in 1873 is still on the property which is frequently visited by bear, elk herd, mule deer and occasionally a moose or two can be found swimming in the pond west of the ranch headquarters. The ranch is located 5,000 feet below the summit of nearby Pikes Peak (Tava) and this tree is situated along the south side of an old trail that lies on the route between Crystal Peak and Pikes Peak. This Ute Prayer Tree has definite ligature marks where it was staked to the ground and what appears to be a deliberate cut in the underside of the thick bark where pine pitch still seeps and hardens. There are many medicinal and practical uses of this pine pitch, including being used for herbal teas, as an adhesive or even for a fire starter. One of the most intriguing aspects of this tree, beyond its impressive 360° distortion of the trunk, is its location. If one were to leave the old trail, visible in the photo directly behind the Trailmarker Tree, then head south towards the summit of Pikes Peak, they cross a nearby draw and as they come up the other side they come across the opening to an abandoned mine. This mine was worked as a gold mine over a century and a half ago and the mine shaft sits atop a white quartz mineral deposit that protrudes upward from the ground. A quartz crystal or other small gem stones were often collected along the route of a vision quest and left by the Ute tribal member as an offering to their Creator who was believed to reside in a cloud tepee on top of Pikes Peak. This Ute Trailmarker Tree has stood at this location for perhaps over two hundred years and may have guided countless Ute Indians as they made their ascension towards the summit of the Ute's most sacred mountain Tava.

Crystal Peak: This photo is of Crystal Peak, which is located a few miles north of the small town of Florissant, Park County, Colorado. Several older Ute Prayer Trees, including Trailmarkers and Burial Trees, have been located at this historic location. One Ute Burial Tree with an impressive view of Tava (Pikes Peak) was discovered pointing towards Tava with two white quartz rocks placed on top of the horizontal trunk running parallel to the ground. Another memorable Ute Prayer Tree was discovered just below the summit with a deep claw mark of a large bear. The Ute were known to have collected amazonite (small blue colored gem stones) and smoky quartz crystals which they carried to the top of Tava to leave as an offering to the Creator. Both Ute men and women were encouraged to take at least one vision quest during their lifetime to the top of Tava to seek wisdom and spiritual enlightenment from their Creator. These vision quests often lasted several days and were undertaken during a time of fasting where the Ute would not ingest in any food or water, which was intended to strengthen their personal commitment while deepening their spiritual journey. Deep mediation, personal chants and individual songs often accompanied their prayers which were internally focused, seeking guidance, for example, on what the Creator intended for them in living their lives. Crystal Peak is today located on private property and this photo was taken and is being included in this publication with the consent of the land owner. This photo is taken facing to the west and just below where this photo was taken stands the family cabin near an artesian mountain spring.

Chapter 8 - The Ute Must Return
There is no greater honor for a warrior than to die bravely in battle defending one's tribe.

Following the Battle of Milk Creek or what would tragically become known as the Meeker Massacre; Colorado Governor Frederick Walter Pitkin concluded his congressional testimony by shaking his fist in the air and shouting, *"The Utes Must Go!"* This quote became a rallying cry that could be heard echoing throughout the Shining Mountains. No doubt it sounded better than the underlining motive, "We Want That Land!" When the newly elected Governor Pitkin arrived in Washington on Monday January 26, 1880, he went to work portraying all the Ute as, *"uncivilized, savage, roaming nomads"* who he believed could not be civilized.

Governor Pitkin did reveal the real issue with the "Ute Problem" was that the Ute were, "…an impediment to the opening of the best lands in the State…the mineral wealth of the unsettled part," and referred to the size of Colorado's Mineral Belt spreading across the 12,000,000 acre Ute Reservation west of the Continental Divide as "exceedingly great." Pitkin described Nathan Meeker or Father Meeker, as, "well known all over the country as a pure and genuine philanthropist." Pitkin complained that the White River chiefs were so ungrateful of Father Meeker's benevolent efforts that they had asked him (Governor Pitkin) to remove Meeker and assign them some other Indian Agent.

Reading Governor Pitkin's words brings many questions into play. First, had he complied with the chiefs' request to appoint the White River Ute a new Indian Agent, could the Battle of Milk Creek that claimed the life of Major Thomas Tipton Thornburgh and 12 of his troops, along with an estimated 19 to 27 Ute, been avoided? And if so, would not the death of Nathan Meeker, along with the ten men who were his employees at the White River Indian Agency in western Colorado, also have been avoided? Could any part of Governor Pitkin's vindictive attitude against all the Ute bands been driven in part for a desire to shift the blame away from himself for having the Meeker incident occur during his term as Governor, remembering the previous Governor had been fired due to the Sand Creek Massacre? And lastly, did his desire that the Ute leave Colorado have anything to do with the mineral wealth lying beneath the Ute Reservation?

The Washington Post assumed an unpopular stand against the anti-Ute sentiment, unpopular in Colorado anyway, stating, "There is a strong disposition, in some quarters, to hold a whole tribe responsible for the crimes of a few of its members. It would be as reasonable and humane to call for the hanging of all the citizens of Washington because murders and brutal outrages on women have been perpetrated here, many of the outrages of which Gen. Pitkin complains were caused by failure to deliver their food when it was needed. Of course this repudiation and failure on the part of the Government does not justify murder, let us try to deal fairly with those who have committed no crimes."

Back in Colorado, the local San Juan pioneers took a different stance, as evident in the Ouray newspaper called the *Solid Muldoon*. David Day wrote, "The Ute are highly pleased with Washington. Well, we are perfectly willing they should stay there." Regardless of one's position at the time or even today, the result would remain the same: despite Chief Ouray's efforts to hold on to their land granted to the Ute under previous treaties with the government, on August 27, 1881, his widow, Chipeta, would join the 1,458 other Ute who were escorted by the military out of Colorado into the Utah Territory. Newspapers across Colorado reported the mass exodus under the headlines, "The Utes Have Gone."

The Ute who may have been the original indigenous people in Shining Mountains were the last Native Americans in Colorado forced onto a reservation. A tribal elder commented at the time that there had been so many atrocities committed by both sides upon one another that complete forgiveness would not be made in his lifetime, nor his son's lifetime or his grandson's lifetime. He predicted it would not be until the seventh generation had been born until all hateful feelings could finally be set aside to allow the healing to begin. This reference to the seventh generation may have been derived from the Constitution of the Iroquois Nations; The Great Binding Law, which states, "In every deliberation, we must consider the impact on the seventh generation…even if it requires having skin as thick as the bark of a pine." The seventh generation, approximately 140 years, is now upon us.

Benjamin Franklin, one of the Founding Fathers of the United States, sat in council with the Iroquois Nation and was said to have been so impressed with their Constitution that he emulated portions of their Constitution when helping to frame the Constitution of the United States. In particular, it is believed Franklin was so fascinated with their concept of a separation of government, that the three branches of government in the United States, the Executive, Legislative and Judicial branches of government was adopted from the Iroquois Constitution.

The Ute, like many other Native American Indian Tribes, believe that a vision may reveal itself in any form: a spirit may send a messenger; the vision could be communicated by a sign or communicated by words, either seen or heard. The Lakota have a term for these words, "hanbloglaka", which means "visionary language." According to Arthur Versluis, the author of *Sacred Earth, The Spiritual Landscape of Native America*, the words of hanbloglaka, this visionary language, can be understood by the holy man.

I am keenly aware that I have more than my fair share of faults and do not in any way wish to profess myself a holy man or widely proclaim to have had a vision. That said I do wish to humbly share an interesting experience which does seem somewhat intertwined with this story of the Ute Indian Prayer Trees. While hiking with my dog and two friends along an old Native

American Indian Trail in the Black Forest, undoubtedly traveled by the Ute, I became aware of an overwhelming thought, a need to "invite the Ute to a BBQ." One might have hope for a more meaningful piece of wisdom, perhaps learning the meaning of life or maybe six winning Powerball numbers. But that was all there was, just those six words.

Part of the challenge was that I didn't personally know any Ute. Within a month or so, I found myself on the Southern Ute Reservation on June 25, 2013, standing alongside my two friends, Vern Kuykendall and Phil Tinsley, shaking hands with Ute Tribal Elder Dr. James Jefferson and Nathan Strong Elk, Acting Executive Director of the Southern Ute Cultural Center and Museum in Ignacio, Colorado. Over the course of the discussion about the Ute Indian Prayer Trees of the Pikes Peak Region, the invitation was extended to the Ute to come to El Paso County see these trees and have "a BBQ."

This "BBQ", scheduled for August, was to be the first gathering of the Ute, intended to reconnect them to the UPTs cultivated by the Tribal Ancestors in the Black Forest 150-350 years ago, nearly didn't happen. On June 11, 2013 a forest fire broke out on Shoup Road, east of Highway 83, just a few miles west of La Foret the conference center where the Ute gathering was to be held. This raging wildfire claimed the lives of two El Paso County residents trapped in the inferno while trying to evacuate their beloved home north of La Foret. By the time the fire was finally contained a week and a half later, it burnt more than 14,000 acres and caused more than $85 million in damages to property and completely destroyed 486 homes. The Black Forest Fire would be declared the most destructive fire in Colorado's history, surpassing the deadly Waldo Canyon Fire of just the previous year.

The Black Forest Fire destroyed homes directly across the street from La Foret and burnt the trees and scorched grass right up to the north edge of the pavement across from the front gate of La Foret, located at 6145 Shoup Road. Everyone who worked or lived anywhere near La Foret agreed it was a miracle that not one tree on La Foret's heavily treed, 400 plus acreage was touched by the fire that raged out of control for ten days. La Foret had originally been the summer home of Alice Bemis Taylor and her husband Frederick Morgan Pike Taylor, one of the most prominent families in early Colorado Springs, were well-known for their generous history of philanthropy including the construction of the Colorado Springs Fine Arts Center.

The Taylor's had no children of their own, but had adopted a daughter, Doree, who never married and had no children of her own. Mr. Taylor had died in 1929, and Mrs. Taylor passed away in 1942, leaving a trust fund to care for her daughter for the rest of her life and bequeathed La Foret to the Colorado Congregational Church, known today as the Rocky Mountain Conference of the United Church of Christ.

Two intriguing things happened just before the Black Forest Fire broke out; the first was after five years without hearing anything from the law firm in New York, an attorney who had served as executor for the Bemis Taylor trust fund called the then Executive Director of La Foret, Ralph Townsend. The attorney from New York explained that the only heir to the Bemis Taylor family, Doree had passed away. He explained she had lived a long life and had been cremated upon her passing. Doree's ashes were still in the possession of the law firm in New York City. After some consideration, the law firm felt the one place where Doree might rest in peace was at La Foret, and he wanted to know if La Foret would allow him to bring Doree's ashes to be scattered on the grounds there. Ralph said that was the least they could do since La Foret wouldn't exist had it not been for the generosity of Doree's mother, Alice Bemis Taylor.

When the attorney arrived with Doree's ashes at La Foret, he brought something rather unexpected: a pair of hand-carved wooden bears that had been crafted by an unknown artist likely in the 1920s. Old photography showed these at one time had rested on the mantelpiece above the fireplace in the Taylor's summer home, today known as the Ponderosa Lodge. Doree's ashes were sprinkled over the grounds at La Foret under the Ponderosa Pines. Those two wooden bears, measuring about sixteen inches in length, were replaced where they once stood nearly a hundred years earlier on the mantel above the fireplace and were present throughout our indoor meetings during the first UPT Retreat two months after the deadly Black Forest Fire.

The second amazing occurrence that happened about a week later, approximately one week prior to the Black Forest fire, was a moose started showing up on La Foret. Ralph Townsend said deer were frequent visitors at La Foret; however, this was the first time a moose had ever been seen on the property. People who had lived in El Paso County for over fifty years had never seen a moose in the Black Forest. On the first night of the UPT Retreat as the Ute began arriving the most beautiful female moose made a surprise appearance along the left bank of Kettle Creek and stood for some time, almost as a sentry welcoming the Ute home. After the moose had moved away the area around where she was standing was explored and a previously unknown Ute Trailmarker Tree was discovered within twenty feet from where she was standing.

I was present when Ralph Townsend told the story to Dr. Jefferson about Doree's ashes and the return of the wooden bears. Ralph further explained how the moose showed up every morning for the week prior to the fire and asked if Dr. Jefferson thought there might be any connection. Without any hesitation, Dr. Jefferson replied, *"absolutely,"* explaining that these events were not disconnected, random activities. He explained that, *"As I see it, the bears and the moose were sent by the Creator as protectors for the trees"* and described how the Creator used the wind, through his breath, to become the breath of the moose and the two bears which directed the fire away from La Foret's sacred trees.

I was reluctant to include this story in this book; however, I remain somewhat at a loss how to otherwise explain how the wind for ten straight days blew out of the south, keeping the fire from spreading across the street into the tall Ponderosa Pines at La Foret. This is especially puzzling since the prevailing winds in this region are almost always out of the north. What complicated my decision to include the mention of the moose and the bears when normally it has not been my intent to push my views or beliefs on anyone, is my desire to report the information I gathered from people and things and allow the reader to make up his or her own mind about the spirituality of the Ute sacred trees.

One other weather related story found in historical records is retold in the conclusion of the book *Sacred Earth, The Spiritual Landscape of Native America*, by Arthur Versluis. The story relates, "On a turbulent Friday evening in April 1991, a tornado was headed directly for the city of Maple Hill, Kansas, a little town just west of Topeka. A powerful tornado, it had just destroyed a number of buildings and as moving directly for the village when, as the local newspaper reported, 'Buffalo Mound, a hill just west of the town, diverted the twister to the north. It was on the ground within a quarter mile of the town,' volunteer fireman Jim Puff said, 'We were just awful lucky.' Or one might take into account that Buffalo Mound, the highest point for many miles, was also sacred to the Indian tribes and was a site to which one went for fasting and praying." Perhaps La Foret was simply blessed with favorable winds or prior mitigation efforts or heroic efforts by the first responders, all of which are true or maybe, it too was "awful lucky."

From earlier research, I was familiar with the Ute's belief that the wind is the breath of the Creator and one of his many gifts. I have also come to know from discussions with several Ute that many believe they have a personal protector, a spirit that keeps them from harm and keeps them from being afraid. Dr. Jefferson shared his belief his protector kept him alive during the Korean War and although he did not know his protector by name, he had seen his image many times and knew he was an Indian man, possibly one of his Grandfathers. He shared a story of how during the War another soldier had also seen Dr. Jefferson's protector, sitting on a wall, and asked Dr. Jefferson if he knew he was there. Dr. Jefferson replied he knew he was always there watching over him.

La Foret (La Foret is a French word meaning The Forest), has adopted as their motto, "Keep the Spirit Alive" and is a conference retreat destination that serves all religious denominations as an educational and non-profit organization, complete with overnight cabins, dining hall and meeting rooms. This venue turned out to be an excellent choice to host the first Ute Prayer Tree Retreat. Their acceptance of people with other spiritual beliefs, their beautiful view of Pikes Peak, plus the fact they are fortunate to have on property dozens of the most amazing UPTs in all of the Pikes Peak Region, made for a wonderful three day venue for the Ute and our host committee members.

On August 25, 2013, just two months after shaking hands with Dr. Jefferson for the first time on the Southern Ute Reservation, we met again at the La Foret Conference and Event Center in El Paso County. As Nathan Strong Elk would later write "For the next three days we searched for those values we share in common. Beliefs that unite us, not divide us, most especially was a dedication for the future education, appreciation and preservation of the Ute Indian Prayer Trees of the Pikes Peak Region, so that future generations may view these Culturally Modified Trees, and use them to better understand the past, evaluate the needs of present, and communicate a shared vision of the preferred future."

There were many highlights over our three days we spent together, sharing our understanding of the various varieties of Ute Prayer Trees and discussing what our research had so far revealed. One of the experiences we appreciated was just how welcomed the Ute were wherever we went throughout El Paso County. At the invitation of several land owners, we visited many UPTs on private property and shared hikes together at La Foret and in Fox Run Park to explore the UPT located at those two locations. While at Fox Run, the Gleneagle Women's Hiking Club hosted a picnic lunch for the Ute guests, and on the last day we visited the volunteer staff at the Old Colorado City Historical Society (OCCHS) who hosted a much appreciated crock pot luncheon.

Over lunch, the OCCHS Archivist, Tom Daniels, shared several photos of the Ute he had copied from their extensive photo archives. Tom had arranged these photos with captions describing each of the photos, professionally organized on a large poster-board positioned on an easel. One of these photos titled The Last Shan Kive September 3rd, 1913 Garden of the Gods drew particular attention of several of the Ute guests. This black and white landscape photo showed 56 individuals, most of them Ute men, women and a few children, with a few tepees erected behind them and the unmistakable rock formations in the background of the Garden of the Gods.

The Last Shan Kive photo was dated 1913 and is one that is fairly well known among local historians. It froze a significant moment in time where 53 Ute were gathered to be photographed for an important occasion, evidenced by them being dressed in their finest traditional clothing: most of the men were adorned with magnificent feathered headdresses. This photo was included in Irving Howbert's 1914 book *The Indians of the Pike's Peak Region, Including an Account of the Battle of Sand Creek, and of Occurrences in El Paso County, Colorado, during the War with the Cheyennes and Arapahoes, in 1864 and 1868.* This book contains the beautiful 1913 landscape photo and numbered across the bottom from 1 to 56 are the names of the individual that appears in the photo above the number.

Most of the Ute were identified with the corresponding name next to the number although a few were described then labeled "unknown" and two of the only three white men standing on the left and right of the formation were also marked as "unknown." Someone, a hundred and fifty years ago, had painstakingly captured the names of most of the people in the photo, most importantly the Ute people who were present. When looking at the faces of the people who are depicted in this historic old photograph all of whom have now passed on, one cannot help but wonder if this is perhaps the one and only photo ever taken of many of them? Perhaps this is the only photo that survives to give proof of their existence on this earth, not unlike the Ute Prayer Trees sprinkled across the Pikes Peak Region.

While preparing for the Ute's visit to the Old Colorado City History Center scheduled for August 28, 2013, archivist Tom Daniels and I had chatted briefly about how nice it would be if our Ute guests could help us identify some of the people in the photos, the ones who were marked unknown, hoping we might even find one or two that might be related. During lunch on the day of our Ute visit to OCCHS, I couldn't help noticing the interest they demonstrated with Tom's photo display especially the Last Shan Kive landscape photo. Finally, my curiosity got the best of me and I approached Nathan Strong Elk and asked what the buzz was about.

Nathan Strong Elk explained that they had this exact photo on the reservation at the Southern Ute Cultural Center and Museum; however, the legend at the bottom had been cut off. They knew many of the people in the photo were likely their relatives, but until this very moment, they didn't know who was who, which ones were their relatives. This may have been the first time some of the Ute present at this casual lunch, just a short distance from the Garden of the Gods, saw what their great or perhaps great-great grandparents actually looked like.

It was a heartwarming moment to realize that instead of us learning who a few unknown individuals were in the photos, Tom Daniels and the OCCHS had instead reunited potentially dozens of living Ute from the Southern Ute Reservation with their Ute tribal ancestors. It was not lost on any of us that this year, 2013, was the 100 year anniversary of the last Shan Kive when this photo was taken in a sacred place of the Ute, the Garden of the Gods. Out of respect for those Ute who had gathered here in 1913, for the fifteen Ute guests (10 adults and 5 children) who attended the first Ute Indian Prayer Tree Retreat in 2013 and for future Ute generations, we include that picture and a list of those names in the historic photo in this book.

Reading the names above while looking around the room at the descendants of the Ute in the photograph and thinking of those I had privilege to meet on the Southern Ute Reservation during research on Prayer Trees, really made history come alive. Many of the people I have met, including Dr. James Jefferson, Austin Box, Erwin Taylor, and four year old Nakai Box, are direct descendants of many of the Ute in this photo who helped shape our collective history and culture.

As with our UPT project, this photograph serves as a gentle reminder: the study of the Ute Indian Prayer Trees is not simply a study of the trees, but more importantly, it's about the People behind the trees. In a memorable act of kindness and in the spirit of generosity that repeated itself throughout the Ute's first gathering in perhaps a hundred years at the base of their most sacred mountain, I watched as Tom Daniels handed the photo display to Nathan Strong Elk for him to take back to the reservation with him so that other Ute may also identify their Tribal ancestors from the legend at the bottom of the photo. As the Ute were leaving OCCHS that afternoon, Tom whispered to me that he could always make another photo display, besides I knew for him this is what being a photo archivist is all about, reuniting the past with the present so it can be retained and shared with others in the future, sort of like our UPT project.

"The Ute must return, not because this land belonged to them, but because they belonged to this land." - John Wesley Anderson

The landscape photograph above was taken at the last Ute Shan Kive in Garden of Gods (circa 1913). The photo is of 56 people. Most were Ute and were identified by name in a type-written caption below the photo. The original photographer was Clarence Coil of Colorado Springs. This photo is published courtesy of the Special Collections of the Pikes Peak Library District (PPLD). (Photo divided for better viewing).

Shan Kive 1913 Ute Indian Camp, Garden of the Gods - photo by Clarence Coil

1.   Tod Powell.
2.   Unknown.
3.   Henry Box, in front of tent.
4.   Henry Box, Jr. the boy holding a hat.
5.   Steve Burch, the tall Indian by tent.
     A full blood Navajo and grandfather of Dorothy Burch Box.
6.   Bob Richards, late a judge at Ignacio, Colo.
7.   Indian above blanket on ground is unknown.
8.   Tony Buck, son of Buckskin Charlie, lately living at Ignacio, Colo.
9.   Henry Jackson, also called Myole. A full blood Comanche captured by the Ute.
     He wears the otter skin over his shoulder.

10. *Alice Grove, a Northern Ute. Woman in plaid shawl.*

11. *Man in back is an unknown Northern Ute.*

12. *Woman wearing paisley shawl unknown Northern Ute.*

13. *An unknown old Northern Ute.*

14. *Lady in striped shawl is Lucy Bent, aunt of Eddie Box.*

15. *Na-Nice or Norris, a Ute from Ignacio.*

16. *Lucy Cloud (little girl).*

17. *Large woman with long braids is Emma Naulr, wife of Buckskin Charlie.*

18. *Man in front of tepee is Moab.*

19. *Child in front of Moab not known.*

20. *Lady with hair not braided is Drake, T. Newton's mother-in-law.*

21. *George Tree, wearing a striped scarf. Father of Jo Tree.*

22. *Man with breast shield and tomahawk unknown.*

23. *Lady with long braids is Minnie Cloud.*

24. *Man with cuffs and long hair is Isaac Cloud.*

25. *Lady with large earrings is Kuebler.*

26. *Man with scarf holding blanket is unknown.*

27. *Child is Anna Price Silva.*

28. *Lady with hair over one eye is Sarah Price.*

29. *Man with white band on headdress unknown.*

30. *Woman with decorated blouse unknown.*

31. *Man with white headdress and chin band unknown.*

32. *The widow of Chief Ouray, venerable Chipeta.*

33. *Woman with decorated blouse unknown.*

34. *Buckskin Charlie, with feather in his hand, a mustache and a beaded belt.*
35. *Woman with long hair & bows is Irana, wife of Tony Buck, daughter-in-law of Buckskin Charlie.*
36. *Jim Bush.*
37. *Lady with bearclaw necklace is Anna Bush.*
38. *Man with fur around sleeves, is John Taylor.*
39. *Unknown woman.*
40. *Unknown child.*
41. *Man with white apron unknown.*
42. *Woman with dentalia, large sleeves, is unknown.*
43. *Man in front of tepee unknown.*
44. *Child unknown.*
45. *Man in white at end of tepee unknown.*
46. *Martha Tree Lucero.*
47. *Northern Ute, unknown.*
48. *Woman with long hair and circular design on shawl is Sally Box.*
49. *Unknown boy.*
50. *Na-nice or Norris, wife with neat double braids.*
51. *Jo Price in front of tepee.*
52. *Holding list cloth, Edwin Cloud, father of Sunshine Cloud Smith, Grandfather of Mrs. Box.*
53. *Eddie Box or Harry Richards or Jim Cloud (identity uncertain).*
54. *Kuebler's Grandmother.*
55. *Unknown man.*
56. *Unknown man.*

Dr. Jefferson in the San Juan National Forest: This photo was taken by the author of Dr. James M. Jefferson, Southern Ute Tribal Elder, while searching for sacred Ute Prayer Trees at Turkey Springs, in the San Juan National Forest. This portion of the San Juan National Forest is located northwest of Pagosa Springs, Colorado. The San Juan National Forest covers more than 1,878,846 acres (2,935.7 sq mi or 7,603.42 km) and occupies land in Archuleta, Conejos, Dolores, Hinsdale, La Plata, Mineral, Montezuma, Rio Grande, San Miguel and San Juan Counties. It also borders the Uncompahgre National Forest to the north and the Rio Grande National Forest to the east. The forest contains two alpine wilderness areas; the South San Juan, Piedra and Weminuche Wilderness Areas. Weminuche is a Ute word meaning the People who have gone before. Dr. Jefferson holds a PhD in linguistics and coauthor of The Southern Ute, A Tribal History. Dr. Jefferson is a veteran of the Korean War and lives on the Southern Ute Reservation, Ignacio, Colorado. Dr. Jefferson is the grandson of Southern Ute Chief Severo who was a sub-chief under Chief Ouray. Dr. Jefferson can trace his Ute lineage to both the Capote and Tabegauche Ute Band however he always adds, "If you go back far enough we are all related." Recent DNA evidence has suggested that Dr. Jefferson is correct with this assertion. This photo was taken of Dr. Jefferson on the morning June 21st, 2014.

Old Ute Chiefs Burial Tree: This set of three intertwined trees are located on BLM land near Turkey Springs, in the San Juan National Forest, northwest of Pagosa Springs, Colorado. This living sculpture is an extraordinary example of the advanced horticulture knowledge, skill and ability resident at one time within the Ute culture. The younger Ponderosa Pine with the darker bark has been transplanted and grafted onto the larger and older of the three trees. The height, girth and nearly full orange color of the bark of the largest tree are consistent with similar Ponderosa pines in this forest with tree ring counts establishing these trees are well over 300 years old. The younger tree wraps around the older tree then bridges the gap over to the third tree and is estimated to be less than 200 years old. Notice about two feet above the ground where three metal rods have been inserted through each tree in effect pinning the first two on the right together. The bark on the third tree has been split to allow the younger tree to grow into and fuse with the tree on the left. Nearby are other Ute Prayer Trees, multiple fire pits and burial mounds, indicating this area was a sacred site for the Ute Nation. These trees were discovered in the Weminuche Wilderness area by Patti Brady, a National Forest Park Ranger and Erwin Taylor, a highly respected Southern Ute Tribal Elder. This intertwined tree formation was referred to as the Old Ute Chiefs Burial Tree by two Southern Ute Elders. When asked why, both Elders replied they didn't know or couldn't say and shrugged their shoulders. This is a response I have often encountered when probing for details from Tribal Elders, particularly if the subject was concerning a sacred Ute ceremony or sacred site. I have come to respect this polite reply as a way of indicating my questions were becoming a little too sensitive. This photo was taken on June 21st, 2014, the morning of the summer solstice.

Arborglyph: This rare Ute Arborglyph was discovered in the Turkey Springs area of the San Juan National Forest, northwest of Pagosa Springs, Colorado. Similar to a petroglyph, an arborglyph is a carving of the tree bark to communicate a message or a story. This remarkable arborglyph uses a sculpting technique known as a relief or relieve rilievo which is a Latin verb meaning to raise and is sometimes referred to by the French term; bas-relief. This sophisticated sculpting technique gives the impression the image has been raised when in fact the image has been cut away from the background which was actually lowered. Sculpture is a branch of the visual arts represented by three-dimensional images or figures; remarkably this arborglyph is evidence of an intelligent advanced culture that also understood archaeoastronomy. Archaeoastronomy is the study of how people in the past "have understood the phenomena in the sky, how they used these phenomena and what role the sky played in their culture." The Ute People possessed a vast understanding of the solstice and equinox alignments, as well as the Pleiades Star Cluster known as the Seven Sisters. Several Ute Prayer Trees found today through the Shining Mountains have celestial alignments and this arborglyph is believed to be connected to the summer solstice. At the base of this tree, about 12 inches above ground level, is an unnatural horizontal indentation that encircles the entire tree. The image of a man's foot can be seen touching this indentation just to the left of the midpoint of the photo and the carving is so detailed the toes can even be counted and his heal is clearly visible. Above the ankle of the left leg his calf and thigh are visible and the man's right leg can be seen in the background. Above and to the left of these legs that appear to be walking is the profile of man's head leaning forward and facing to left (east). The details of a man's left eye, jaw line and what appear to be either braids or a feather extends downward from the back of his head. Studying the background around the leg area, other legs can be observed and gives the impression of people walking on a trail to the east. Approximately 10" to the left of the man's left leg, on the wood beneath the bark extending the length of his body, the wood appears to be sunken allowing the morning sunlight to highlight the man's leg. The nearby trail leads to the natural hot springs in Pagosa Springs, then travels to the east and circles north towards the Black Forest and high plains beyond where the annual bison hunts took place. This photo was taken by the author on June 21st, 2014 the morning of the summer solstice.

Walk in Fox Run with the Trees: *This photo was taken in Fox Run Regional Park, located in northern El Paso County, Colorado. The photo was shot following a picnic hosted by the Gleneagle Women's Hiking Club for 15 members of the Southern Ute Reservation during the first Ute Indian Prayer Tree Retreat hosted at La Foret in 2013. The purpose of the retreat was to reconnect the Ute people of today with the Ute Prayer Trees that were modified by their tribal ancestors. A special effort was made during the retreat to collect the wisdom of the Elders and focus attention towards saving this vanishing piece of Ute culture for their children who have recently been born, the Seventh Generation. This photo shows Carol and Samantha walking hand-in-hand down an old trail to visit a group of sacred prayer trees. One of the most spectacular Ute Prayer Trees found in the Black Forest, a rare Prophecy Tree, is located directly ahead on their right and several nearby Ute Prayer Trees point towards where this Hugging Tree can be found today. Fortunately Jeremy Symes, El Paso County Park Supervisor and his employees are very familiar with Ute Indian Prayer Trees and are committed to ensuring these sacred trees are protected so that they can be appreciated by many future generations.*

Chapter 9 - Conclusion The Dream of the Elders
Seek the Póogats, experts who have been there before,
they know the way you wish to go.

Since the Ute believe nothing is random, that everything in life is intertwined, that there are no coincidences, I believe that my last day of field research may have been chosen for me. The date, location and the people I was with does seem to have been more than simply good fortune. I found myself on the Southern Ute Reservation in Ignacio, Colorado, watching the reddish orange sunrise on the morning of June 21, 2014, the day of the summer solstice.

Like many other cultures around the world, the Ute were intimately aware that a solstice occurs twice a year when the sun reaches its highest or lowest point in the sky marking the precise midpoint of either the summer or winter. The equinoxes are the two dates of the year in the spring and fall when daylight and darkness are approximately equal. The solstices and equinoxes served the Ute to mark the coming and passing of these annual events, year after year, season after season. The Ute accepted these events as another gift that they had been given from the Creator, a celestial calendar.

Since the beginning of time, the Ute people have always tried to live in harmony with the world around them and the universe above them. The summer solstice, sometimes called midsummer, gave me the one day of the year with the longest period of sunlight. This solar event, tracing the path of the sun as it rises to traverse across the sky from east to west, has been studied by ancient peoples around the world; the most well-known are perhaps the people who gather at *Stonehenge* in England to celebrate the rising of the sun over what is known as the Heal Stone positioned to the east of the round megalithic structure.

The Ute were known to study the path of the sun as it rose on the eastern horizon and set in the west. However; they, didn't traditionally build stone monuments to mark the rising or setting sun, the Creator had taken care of that for them by placing them in the Shining Mountains and surrounding them with tall trees. The Ute would have to learn where their traditional migration routes and campsites were in relation to the sun or moon or stars, from the Peogats, the elders who had been there before, season after season. The Peogats were the experts and knew the way in which the Nuche wanted to go throughout the Shining Mountains to find food and fresh water. The elders knew the best places to camp, how long to stay, when to move on and how to be guided by the sun and the trees.

The Ute planned their migration routes throughout the Shining Mountains, keenly aware that with the passing of each day, sunlight would grow longer, then shorter at midsummer, and that fall would eventually lead to winter. The survival of the Tribe, the Nuche, would depend on how well prepared they were to sustain themselves throughout the winter months. The winter solstice occurs on either December 20, 21 or 22, and marks the longest night of the year. The Ute also knew to use their winter months wisely in preparation of the coming spring when they would begin anew on their annual migration route usually in a counter-clockwise direction, starting from the lower and warmer regions then moving in to the higher and colder mountainous regions.

During our many discussions and hikes across the forested areas of El Paso, Teller, Douglas, Alamosa, Park and Custer Counties, I have come to know and respect Dr. James Jefferson immensely, for his undying commitment to our UPT "Mission" to reconnect the Ute back to these sacred trees and the trees back to the Ute nation, and to make certain I, as a recorder of our research, had my facts correct. Dr. Jefferson was never shy about speaking up when necessary and I valued his role as a Ute Tribal Elder to speak out about something so as to set the record right.

One such teaching moment came during a meeting when I made reference to the agenda for the second annual UPT gathering at La Foret in the Black Forest. The agenda was flexible I said, since we were on Indian Time, implying we would start the event whenever we got around to it. Dr. Jefferson was offended; as he should have been by my assuming something I had heard about the Native American culture and applied this misperception to all Native American cultures, especially to that of the Ute. Dr. Jefferson was not shy in letting me know that when he or any Ute told you something, he meant it.

As my research continued I found several references for where the Ute men were known for being on time, and throughout their long history, the Ute warriors in particular were known for always keeping their word. Dr. Jefferson emphasized his point by stating, *"If I told you I would meet you at a certain pass at sunup, I would be there."* Sadly, I had fallen into the same trap as so many others, especially the early pioneers. Don't judge the Ute by the actions of other Native American tribes or perceptions that might not be true; the Ute have their own distinct cultural values and punctuality is one of those values.

This misperception of time being an approximate or unimportant point, on my part, was to Dr. Jefferson a point of personal and cultural pride on his part, one that was consistently confirmed throughout the historical record. In Val FitzPatrick's book *Red Twilight, The Last Free Days of the Ute Indians,* he writes about his first-hand account and relates stories told to him by others of the last free days of the Ute. Valentine Stewart Parnell FitzPatrick or Val as he was remembered by his friends, was born January 4, 1886 in a log cabin near a silver mine outside of Georgetown, Colorado. He lived his entire life in Colorado's northwest, until his death on July 3, 1988, at the age of 102. The FitzPatrick homestead was not far from the Uintah and Ouray Indian Reservation established in 1861, under President Abraham Lincoln's administration.

FitzPatrick's book describes how the earliest Ute (Noochew) lived in different family groups, *"before non-Indians came. These bands were spread out through Utah, Colorado, Wyoming, and New Mexico, in an area the size of Texas. The Uintah and Ouray Reservation is the second largest Indian Reservation in the United States and serves as home for the Whiteriver, Uintah, and Uncompahgre bands. Reservations in southern Colorado belong to the Southern and Ute Mountain Utes."* In his book, FitzPatrick confirms what others, including Kit Carson, had noted about the Ute. The men in particular were extremely trustworthy, and if they gave you their word, they kept it. The Ute, especially their leaders, meant what they said and said what they meant.

This lesson also became very clear to me when I had made my third trip to the Southern Ute Reservation, at the invitation of Ute Tribal Elder, Dr. James Jefferson, to meet with a few other Tribal Elders from the Southern Ute and Ute Mountain Ute Reservations, along with a handful of other friends of the Ute. The purpose of our gathering was to share our CMT/UPT research findings and discuss the 2014 Ute Prayer Tree Retreat that would be held August, again at La Foret. One of the Southern Ute Tribal Elders, Erwin Taylor and I had met once before and he and Dr. Jefferson were particularly close friends, as well as respected leaders of the Southern Ute. Also in attendance were two Ute Mountain Ute Tribal Elders, Norman and Glenda Lopez, and Patti Brady, an employee of the U.S. National Park Service who had been assigned to patrol the San Juan National Forest.

The San Juan National Forest is located in the Four Corners area of southwest Colorado and covers a land area of 2,935 square miles, larger than the state of Rhode Island. It had been created by a proclamation signed by the 26th President of the United States, Theodore Roosevelt on June 3, 1905. Riding in President Roosevelt's second inaugural parade, earlier that same year, was the well-respected Ute Chief Yohoovits, Chief Ouray's hand-picked successor known more commonly by his non-Indian name, Buckskin Charlie.

Riding alongside Buckskin Charlie, the last Headman of the Mouache and Capote Indians from the Southern Ute Reservation, rode four other well-known Native American leaders; American Horse, Little Plumb, Hollow Horn Bear and Geronimo. In an article written by Tallias Cantsee of the Ute Mountain Ute Reservation, Ute Elder Alden Naranjo related how, "The leaders of the tribe were selected because of their ability to make decisions…" In the same article, Ute Elder Terry Knight, Sr., was quoted saying, "They were the leaders of the band…they would talk about personal life and how it should be integrated into the sociological system of the tribe…they were actually band Headmen. You remember that…the Old People, the old folks, they had their way of picking their leadership the way their leadership earned their rights…"

Tallias Cantsee's article published in the summer of 2014, by *Travelhost* (Page 59), concluded with words from Dr. James Jefferson describing one of the greatest attributes of Yohoovits was that, "he did not emphatically promote assimilation, quite the opposite, ensuring that tribal ceremonies, events, crafts, language and customs were carried out according to tribal protocol. Yohoovits was adamant about the culture even down to the clothing, wearing men's clothing only at their events. Yohoovits was always concerned with keeping the peace and protecting our interests."

There were probably twenty of us whom Dr. Jefferson had brought together the evening of June 20, 2014, to help plan for the Second Annual Ute Prayer Tree Retreat. I had been asked to share some of our findings regarding sacred trees in the Black Forest, followed by a talk by Patti and Mr. Taylor. Mr. Taylor discussed a fascinating slide presentation showing photos of a sacred Ute site they had visited with Dr. Jefferson two weeks earlier displaying some of the most amazing Ute Prayer Trees I had ever seen. Patti explained how she had to gain permission from her supervisors to escort Mr. Taylor and Dr. Jefferson to this secluded location in the forest.

I was struck by the respect shown by Patti for the Ute people, and for what was no doubt a sacred site marked not only by sacred Ute Prayer Trees, but ancient grave sites of many Ute ancestors. The importance of this site was unknown to the National Park Service until it was brought to their attention by Patti, who is part Cherokee Indian, recognized its importance through previous discussions she had with Dr. Jefferson regarding UPTs. Patti had an early map from 1894 which she had brought with her to the meeting that did show Indian Trails, but it did not mark this site. Patti described how she frequently patrols this general region of the forest, protecting the land from those who would violate federal laws that protect the trees; however, she had only gone to this area on three or four earlier occasions. She described how two weeks ago, she had felt drawn to this area again which lead to discovering this sacred site. When she saw these trees she knew she had to return to show them to Dr. Jefferson and Mr. Taylor.

Mr. Taylor, similar to the other Ute elder men I have been privileged to meet, likes to laugh and often jokes around, usually at my expense being non-Native. During this portion of the discussion he spoke very quietly and very deliberately focused on his presentation. I was impressed by his sincere demonstration of respect for this sacred site, a burial ground for countless generations of his Ute ancestors. I was being guided by one of the Peogats, someone who knew the way in which I wanted to go, who out of trust was showing me not only where, but how to proceed.

The slide presentation included a photograph of an amazing UPT Intertwined Tree, showing a younger tree that had been wrapped around an older, larger Ponderosa, and as it spiraled upward, it crossed to another pine tree a few feet away. Mr. Taylor shared his belief that this tree marked the burial location of an important Ute Chief. The slide presentation also depicted a remarkable UPT Burial Tree with two unmistakable 90 degree bends. I asked Mr. Taylor which direction they pointed. He nodded and confirmed my suspicion, "To the grave sites."

As their slide presentation drew to an end, I turned to Dr. Jefferson, who to my delight, had already asked Patti if she could seek approval from her supervisors to escort me the next day to the San Juan Forest to view these amazing UPTs in person. Her senior management had given Patti their approval to escort me into this area on federal land. We concluded our meeting at the Sky Ute Casino and Resort on Friday evening June 20, 2014, after making arrangements to meet the following morning for breakfast with Dr. Jefferson and Meggan Braley.

Meggan Braley is a personal friend of Dr. Jefferson and as a retired school teacher she was a huge help in organizing and putting on the first Ute Prayer Tree events at La Foret. Although Meggan is not of Ute decent, she does have Native American heritage and a passion for the preservation of all Native American culture and history. After breakfast we departed the reservation and drove to Pagosa Springs. From there we would take one car and follow Patti in her Forest Service truck deep into the Weminuche Wilderness, of the San Juan National Forest.

Filled with excitement, I slept little that night in anticipation of what we might see the following day. I finally drifted off to sleep for a few hours dreaming of what Ute mysteries we might discover waiting us deep in the Weminuche Wilderness. I would not be disappointed. Remembering the words of how the Ute men believed it shameful to allow the morning sun to rise and catch you sleeping "still wrapped in your robes" inside your tepee, I arose before daylight, fixed myself a cup of hot tea, wrapped a wool Indian blanket around my shoulders and watched for the first glint of sunlight to begin to trace the horizon on the eastern sky.

The silhouette of the hilltops and plateaus began to slowly emerge, outlining the eastern edge of the Southern Ute Reservation east of Ignacio, Colorado (named after the famous Ute Chief, Ignacio). The dark drape of a bluish-gray cloud-cover offered the perfect backdrop for the rising sun to reflect the pinkish-orange glow of the early morning's first light. Up this early to witness a sunrise such as this, it is easy to understand why the Ute believe each day is a gift from the Creator, accepting how each gift should be used wisely.

Arriving early for breakfast so as to not keep a Tribal Elder waiting, I found Patti had already secured us a table with hot coffee being poured. We were soon joined by Dr. Jefferson, Meggan Braley, and Doug Knutson, another historian and author of the Old Spanish Trail (which runs across the Southern Ute Reservation, along Ute Indian Trails which existed long before the Spanish stepped ashore on this continent). After breakfast, Doug Knutson headed for New Mexico, and the rest of us made our way to Pagosa Springs, located just 35 miles north of the New Mexico border. This tourist attraction is still known for its beautiful atmosphere and its warm natural hot springs, a favorite rejuvenation destination for the Ute Chief Ouray and countless generations before him over the centuries.

Along the highway leading into Pagosa Springs, Dr. Jefferson and I both spotted several UPTs, the distance from one UPT to the next decreasing as we neared the hot springs. Turning north towards the San Juan National Forest, we followed the paved highway and then turned west into the Weminuche Wilderness area. There off to the south stood a remarkable Trailmarker Tree pointing back to the hot springs at Pagosa. The distinct shape, with one angled bend of the "leader" trunk reaching for the sunlight the primary trunk withering and dying away, was exactly like those that I discovered at the base of Gore Pass in east Vail and back at home deep in the Black Forest.

We arrived at our final destination, deep into the vast forested area of Turkey Springs at just before 10 a.m. Almost immediately upon exiting our vehicles we were all immersed in by the serenity and the peacefulness of this wilderness area, surrounded by mountain peaks to the north and a vibrant green meadow to the west was being fed by a natural spring. Within a few steps of exiting the vehicle with Dr. Jefferson, I found myself in silence under the canopy of tall Ponderosa trees. We had driven past several Ute Indian Prayer Trees of various types including UPT Trailmarkers and Burial Trees before arriving at our final destination in Turkey Springs, but here we were surrounded by the ancients. Ninety foot tall trees, many of them three or four hundred years old, judging by their orange color, gave us ample cool shade as the story of the ancient Ute began to unfold before us, a story of the ancient people who had stood behind these sacred trees.

Clutching his bag of Bull Durham tobacco with its characteristic tan cloth bag and yellow drawstring, Dr. Jefferson, now well into his eighties and slowed considerably by arthritic knees, refused any assistance and walked off to be alone in the tall trees, to make an offering to the ancient ones and offer a prayer of gratitude and hope to the Creator. The distant words of wise counsel I had read from a Native American leader came back to me, in a voice gone quiet long ago, with words from a distant past, but not forgotten: "Do not raise your voice. Do not say anything bad. This place is sacred."

Allowing Dr. Jefferson some private time, I wandered towards an elevated cluster of Juniper and Ponderosa pines, several with definite evidence of being altered by human intervention long ago before any white man had entered these woods. My eyes were drawn to the rock formations, crusted with light green colored dry moss nestled in the yellow green grass. My eyes, now trained to pick out non-natural looking trees or formations of rocks, evidence of having been altered by human hands, spotted ten or twelve rocks neatly arranged in a circle on the ground, with an opening of nearly two feet in diameter – a fire pit! Off to my right, I discovered another grouping of rocks forming another fire ring, then another at the base of a smaller UPT pointing towards the spring off in the valley to our west, past where Dr. Jefferson was performing a tree ceremony.

I had only discovered one Native American fire pit in my previous explorations, but now I was standing on a high ground among these ancient fire rings, literally too numerous to count, surrounded by old Juniper trees and majestic Ponderosas trees. It was not difficult to envision where the Ute had arranged their tepees; here at home in the Shining Mountains. Off to the west the lush grass in the valley would have stood knee deep to their ponies. At the head of the creek, bubbled a spring where the Ute women would have gone to fill their woven water jug, their kenosh, with fresh water each morning, and again several times throughout the day, as the men hunted deer and elk among the beautiful trees that surround this ancient campground.

When it was evident Dr. Jefferson had completed his prayers, I moved closer towards him to see how he was doing, and overhead I spotted the movement of a young eagle in flight, gliding effortlessly. I drew Dr. Jefferson's attention to the graceful presence almost directly above his head and asked if he had seen him. Without looking up, Dr. Jefferson replied with his characteristic smile on his face and twinkle in his eye, "I seen him; he is just checking us out." Dr. Jefferson walked over to rest in the car and after reassuring me he was alright, I rejoined the two ladies intently engaged in conversation around one interesting looking old Ponderosa with an unusual indentation around its base.

Of all the sacred trees we had seen and all the sacred sites we have visited, here was the greatest concentration, largest variety, these were among the most majestic Ute Prayer Trees. Patti Brady and Meggan Braley had been studying one of the largest Ponderosas in this grouping for some time, and as I approached, Patti asked if the Ute ever carved the bark of their Prayer Trees. Keenly aware of the fact I had walked past two Ute Ceremonial Trees to reach the base of the large Ponderosa they had been studying, I answered with caution, "not that I'm aware of" but I knew I was in a scared place of the ancient Ute, the likes of which I had never seen before.

It took some time to understand what we were seeing in this sacred place. Scattered around this site were half a dozen Ute Ceremonial Trees which had their think bark peeled off from one side of the tree. Inside this area where the bark had been peel away fire had been introduced ceremonially to the underlining hard wood. Other than two or three pictures of Ute Ceremonial Trees near Lake George in Teller County that I had come across in treatise written by Jack R. Williams, I had only personally seen one Ute Ceremonial Tree on the Three Eagle Ranch in Douglas County owned by Rollie and Paula Johnson.

"Look," Patti said, "you can see a man walking! There's his leg and his foot, and his other leg." Tracing with a walking stick the outline of the man in the arborglyph carved out of the thick orange bark of the Ponderosa the shape of a man, an Indian man's left leg, could be seen highlighted by the sun's light shining upon his thigh, knee and calf. Extending down to the horizontal indentation that extended completely around the base of the tree, at about 12-14 inches above the ground level, the bark below this line appeared somewhat darker in color. Touching this non-natural line was the man's left foot so clearly recognizable you could count the toes on his left foot as he walked across a trail. Also sculpted in the recessed portion of the trunk that encapsulated the arborglyph was a shape of a large 7-8 foot tall lance point standing upright.

Patti continued to point out the figure's arm, head and feet of at least two other people walking with him: one in front and another one to the rear. She had discovered a Ute Story Tree, a rare Ute Arborglyph! I don't know if the time was exactly 10:51am, the precise moment of the summer solstice that day, but I do know it must have been shortly before 11am when the sunlight shone upon this Arborglyph carved in the bark of this majestic Ponderosa Pine. By sheer coincidence, although Dr. Jefferson teaches there is no such thing, I was able to capture two photos of this sun highlighted arborglyph.

The first arborglyph photo was taken at sometime around 10:00 a.m. shortly after arriving in the Weminuche Wilderness and the image was visible but remained in the shadow of the tree. The second photo was also taken just before 11 a.m. and the image of the man's left leg was clearly highlighted by sunlight making the image of the man walking easier to see. What also came into view were the legs of other people walking from right to left sculpted in the deep orange bark of this old Ponderosa pine tree. This image would have been carved when the tree was much younger, before the Ute were not confined to a reservation. It appears this human event carved in relief into the bark was intended to be seen when it was being illuminating by the sun.

We guessed these trees were at least three hundred years old and were very curious to see just how old the arborglyph tree and the two nearby Ute Medicine and Ceremonial Trees might be as well. Fortunately, we came across the trunk of a nearby Ponderosa that had fallen over and been cut off about four feet from the ground. Noting the orangish color and diameter to be approximately the same as the other large Ponderosas we had come across, I began counting the tree rings as Patti watched. We noticed the pith ring at the very center and several of the innermost rings were somewhat thicker than those found towards the outer bark indicating at the time this tree, and likely most of those that stood around it, had begun to grow during a time blessed with abundant rainfall. Judging from the thinness of many groups of rings, this tree had also withstood many periods of drought during it's over three hundred-year lifespan which extended back to a time before the American Revolution of 1776. One does need to subtract from the total ring count to factor in the age of the tree when the modification occurred. Our best guess was these UPTs may have been between 150-250 years old when they were last culturally modified.

Returning towards where the cars were parked, we came across another very old Ute Medicine Tree. An examination of its ancient bark revealed how the thick bark had been encroaching upon the inner bare bark which was heavily encrusted with harden pine pitch that had seeped from the scar over the years. We discovered two more Ute Ceremonial Trees, one of which actually consisted of four intertwined trees that had been planted or more likely transplanted. A cross sectional view from three feet above ground level would have resembled a four-leaf clover each leaf measuring approximately 18 inches for a total circumference of ten-twelve feet. We wondered if this could be a Medicine Wheel Tree that Dr. Jefferson had mentioned. We observed the bark on the south and north ends had been peeled and both scars showed evidence of scorching from fire being placed against the tree. There had been ancient ceremonies preformed around this tree!

We then drove north and entered the sacred grounds that Erwin Taylor, Patti and Dr. Jefferson had walked two weeks before where they had discovered the ancient grave sites. We stopped and marveled at what had become known as the "Ute Chief Burial Tree." We stood in amazement at how the younger Ponderosa pine had grown out of the base of the older tree, wrapping itself around the older tree until they were fused together as one. Then as it ascended upward and further around the first tree, it crossed a span of approximately four feet and at an upward angle, joined another pine tree as it continued its upward ascension seeking sunlight.

The Ute Leader Ouray died on August 24, 1880, not far west of this wilderness area. I could not help but wonder; could this magnificent Ute Chief Burial Tree have been cultivated in his honor? There was definitely a powerful story here, one of coming from Mother Earth, rising, ascending, uniting, then crossing over to another, joining with another living entity, continuing in a slow steady upward progression, inching ever skyward, year after year, growing towards The Creator. There were undeniably many great Ute Chiefs, including Nevava, Buckskin Charlie, Shavano, Antero and Ignacio. However, Chief Ouray stands alone as having been recognized by many Ute and non-Indians as perhaps the greatest Ute Chief. Born through the union of an Apache father and Ute mother, Ouray became a Tabeguache Ute who dedicated his life to bringing two people, two cultures, together in peace.

Many western historians claim that Ouray was the greatest of all Indian Chiefs and is remembered for his skillful negotiating and peacekeeping abilities. When the Colorado State Capital Building in Denver was built, sixteen stained-glass panels were dedicated to honor sixteen of Colorado's most influential Founding Fathers. Chief Ouray was one of the Native American Indian chosen for this high honor and he was the only individual nominated who received a unanimous vote. It may never be known what Ute Chief Tree or what occasion this tree was altered to honor. This living tribute is truly remarkable evidence of an advanced culture.

My Ute Prayer Tree field research had allowed me the privilege of viewing several hundred Ute Prayer Trees, all across the Rocky Mountains of Colorado, but I had never seen anything like this! On the first large tree, approximately three feet off the ground, long metal rods had been driven partially through the young tree, pinning it to the older tree, and where the younger tree crossed over to the next, at a height of approximately 10-12 feet above the ground, the bark had been peeled away to allow the two trees to fuse together. These three trees had been fused together to form this fascinating single living structure. This was a living ancient artifact sculpted by the strong hands of someone or more likely a people, who possessed the knowledge, skill and ability to culturally modify three trees over a period of several years. This amazing work of art clearly demonstrates a passion to record or honor an event or a person in a most extraordinary way.

Trying to process what we had already been shown; Ute Intertwined Trees, Story Trees, Burial Trees and Ceremonial Trees, I turned to ask Patti where Erwin Taylor had shown her the grave sites. We walked only another 50 yards or so to the north, where we crossed a well-worn dirt trail and entered the area where Patti had been told by Erwin where he "felt people were buried." She began pointing out stacked rock, some more obviously more recent than others. As we descended further into this sacred area, Burial Trees came into view. We found older stacked circular rock formations approximately three to four feet in diameter, many were overgrown with tall grass and wildflowers with their blossoms opened widely, turned to face the sun, absorbing the sunshine. This, the one day of the year with the longest sunlight, would serve as the capstone for all of our collective CMT/UPT research.

From my academic and field research and my prior experience as a homicide detective, I was aware that Native Americans were often buried in shallow graves, curled into a natural fetal position, lying on their side. Rocks were often placed on top of the dirt mound, possibly to mark the location of the grave site or sometimes simply to keep the body from being dug up again by a hungry animal that might smell the decaying flesh. I wondered what might have been buried with the person laying a few feet under the ground, usually a new pair of moccasins for their travels along trails in the afterlife or perhaps a stone tool or a basket for a woman or an unstrung bow and quiver of arrows for a hunter or warrior to use in the happy hunting grounds.

We did see a few more recent graves, recent as in perhaps the mid-twentieth century, one outlined with a rectangular rock formation measuring approximately seven feet in height and two feet in length. At the center of this rock formation stood the weathered stump of a smaller tree. A one-by-six inch unpainted board had been nailed to the top of the stump forming a small T-shape. It was an old grave marker which years ago had displayed the name of the loved one buried beneath the grass and wildflowers at the edge of this quaking Aspen grove.

Southern Ute elder Erwin Taylor had pointed out to Patti the contrasts in the vegetation, in greener color and height of the grass, following the contour of burial sites outlining a circular shaped depression or a mound, indicating the location of where a Ute was buried beneath the dirt. Mother Earth had reclaimed the flesh and blood of the Ute people buried here. The depression where the bodies had once been would hold moisture helping the grass and flowers grow. We took the sacred tobacco Dr. Jefferson had given us and sprinkled the dried leaves of the tobacco over the sites and whispered to those buried here we meant no harm. It was so quiet you could hear the fresh green aspen trees rustling against one another in harmony with the slight breeze, the chatter of unseen birds had shifted in tone from that of alerting others in the forest to the approach of possible danger, to a peaceful, singing to one another, trailing off in the distance muffled by the trees.

Standing one last time before this magnificent old Ute Chief Burial Tree, next to Dr. Jefferson and Meggan, Patti discovered her second diorama of the day; another arborglyph had also been carved into this Ute Prayer Tree. I don't know if it was a lack of lighting or imagination that morning but I was the only one of the four of us who could not make out the image portrayed in this second arborglyph. The harder I looked the more frustrated I became and as we were leaving the forest that day I expressed my disappointment to Dr. Jefferson in having missed seeing this image.

A few days later I received a phone call from Dr. Jefferson who told me he had said a prayer for me to be able to see the images carved into the Old Chiefs Tree. I thanked Dr. Jefferson for his prayer but shared with him that I had already examined all my photos from our trip into the Weminuche Wilderness very carefully and simply had given up seeing anything. Dr. Jefferson replied, "I don't know, it was a pretty powerful prayer."

Later, in studying the photos again I began to see a three dimensional scene: carved in miniature, emerging from the background. As Patti described, it was an image of a woman carrying a small child in the company of a man, the likeness of a Ute family walking across the earth. Similar to the first arborglyph this one was also skillfully carved from the background leaving a three dimensional scene. I was reminded of the words of the sculptor who carved a beautiful image of a bird from stone. When he was asked how he was inspired to carve such a beautiful statue, he simply replied the bird was there all along, all he did was remove the excess stone around the bird to set it free.

Reflecting on the serenity and the sheer beauty of that peaceful place, one begins to worry about the protection of theses sacred places. The graves located in the San Juan National Forest are located on federal land and therefore protected by federal laws, so hopefully they will be preserved for centuries yet to come. Before concluding this book I shared with Dr. Jefferson my conflicting feelings about wanting to write about this sacred yet unknown site and these magnificent Ute Prayer Trees and at the same time protect them. I was comforted by the words of Dr. Jefferson, "Now is the time to take risks, otherwise it will all be forgotten." I had already learned the word "Nuche" in Ute meant "The People" but had to call Dr. Jefferson to ask what the first four letters of the name of the Weminuche Wilderness area meant. He replied "Wemi" applied to the Ute Elders or "The People Who Had Gone Before."

The Ute didn't build churches. The Creator did that for them; the forests were their cathedrals, rocks served as alters, the spires were the trees. Under the guidance of a Ute Spiritual Leader, deep in the Weminuche Wilderness of the San Juan National Forest, our quest for sacred Ute Prayer Trees came full circle. The knowledge of this sacred place and the wisdom passed on through these sacred trees are diminishing with the passing of each generation. But if one opens their hearts and allow their minds to be guided by the Ute Trailmarker Trees, Burial Trees, Medicine Trees, Arborglyphs and Prophecy Trees, the story of the Ute may yet endure to be heard by the Seventh Generation. Sacred trees provide the physical evidence that leads to sacred places; sacred places of the Ute, the People. The Nuche were the people who have gone before, gone but not forgotten.

"Only human failure to find it, study and understand it, can diminish its value."
—Paul L. Kirk. 1953

References & Recommended Reading

1.   Becker, Cynthia S. and Smith, David P., *Chipeta, Queen of the Utes*, A Biography, Western Reflections Publishing Company, Lake City, CO, 2006

2.   Borowsky, Larry, *The Ute Museum, A Capsule History and Guide*, History Colorado, The Colorado Historical Society, Greeley, Colorado, 2009

3.   Broome, Jeff, *Dog Soldier Justice, The Ordeal of Susanna Alderdice in the Kansas Indian War*, University of Nebraska Press, Lincoln, Nebraska, 2003

4.   Butler, William B., *The Fur Trade in Colorado*, Western Reflections Publishing Company, Lake City, CO, 2012

5.   Carson, Phil, Across *the Northern Frontier, Spanish Explorations in Colorado*. Johnson Books, Boulder, Colorado, 1998

6.   Carson, Phil, *Among the Eternal Snows, The First Recorded Ascent of Pikes Peak, July 13-15, 1820*, First Ascent Press, Colorado Springs, Colorado, 1995

7.   Carson, Phil, *Fort Garland Museum, A Capsule History and Guide*, A Museum of The Colorado Historical Society, Denver, CO, 2005

8.   Cleve, Jay PhD., *Path of the Sacred Pipe, Journey of Love, Power, and Healing*, Theosophical Publishing House, Quest Books, Wheaton, IL, 2012

9.   Compton, Ralph, *The Santa Fe Trail, The Old Spanish Trail, The Goodnight Trail*, St. Martin's Paperbacks, 1997

10.   Cunningham, Kevin and Benoit, Peter, *The Ute, A True (Children's) Book*, published by Children's Press, Danbury, CN, 1966

11.   Decker, Peter R., *The Utes Must Go! American Expansion and the Removal of a People*, Fulcrum Publishing, Golden, Colorado, 2004

12.   Densmore, Frances, *How Indians Use Wild Plants for Food, Medicine & Crafts*, Dover Publications Inc., New York, NY, 1974

13. Downes, Dennis with Samors, Neal, *Native American Trail Marker Trees, Marking Paths Through the Wilderness*, Chicago Books Press, Chicago, IL, 2011

14. Douthit, George R. III., *The Boy Who Slept With Bears, A Southern Ute Story*, Rhyolite Press, LLC, Colorado Springs, CO, 2013

15. Eaton, Rachel Caroline, *John Ross and the Cherokee Indians, Native American Leaders*, BiblioLife Antiquarian eBooks, Curating History, The Collegiate Press, George Banta Publishing Company, Menasha, Wisconsin, 1914

16. Ellis, Amanda M., *Pioneers*, The Dentan Printing Company, Colorado Springs, Colorado 1955

17. FitzPatrick, Val, *Red Twilight, The Last Free Days of the Ute Indians*, Yellow Cat Publishing, Yellow Cat Flats, UT, 2000

18. Foster, Dora, *Colorado Yesterdays*, The Dentan Printing Company, Inc., Colorado Springs, CO, 1961

19. Foster, Dora, *Life of First Sheriff, Peak Region Yesterdays*, Colorado Springs Gazette Telegraph, Sunday, May 22, 1960

20. Foster, Dora, *My Childhood Days in Colorado Sunshine*, Dentan-Berkeland Printing Co., Inc., Colorado Springs, CO, 1967

21. Foster, Dora, *Then...The Best of the Pikes Peak Yesterdays*, Dentan Printing Company, Inc., Colorado Springs, CO, 1964

22. Gallagher, Jolie Anderson, *Colorado Forts, Historic Outposts on the Wild Frontier*, The History Press, Charleston, SC, 2013

23. Gray-Kanatiiosh, Barbara A., *Ute, Native Americans (Series)*, Checkerboard Social Studies (Children's) Library, ABDO Publishing Company, Edina, MN, 2004

24. Greene, Jerome A. & Scott, Douglas D., *Finding Sand Creek, History, Archeology, and the 1864 Massacre Site*, University of Oklahoma Press, Norman, OK, 2004

25. Harbour, Midge, *The Tarryall Mountains and the Puma Hills, A History*, Copyright 1982, Third Printing, Colorado Springs, CO October, 2003

26. Hollister, Ovando J., *Colorado Volunteers in New Mexico 1862*, The Lakeside Press, R.R. Donnelley & Sons Company, Chicago, IL Christmas, 1962

27.   Howbert, Irving, *Memories of a Lifetime in the Pike's Peak Region*, Morris Publishing, Nebraska 1925 (reprinted with permission by the Old Colorado City Historical Society, 2007)

28.   Howbert, Irving, *Indians of the Pike's Peak Region*, The Rio Grande Press, Inc., Glorieta, New Mexico, 1914

29.   Hutchens, Alma R, *Indian Herbalogy of North America*, Shambhala Publications, Inc., Boston & London, 1991

30.   Jefferson, James M., Delaney, Robert W. & Thompson, Gregory C., *The Southern Utes, A Tribal History*, Southern Ute Tribe, Ignacio, Colorado, 1973

31.   Jordan, Elaine, *Indian Trail Trees*, Jordan Ink Publishing Company, Ellijay, GA (First printing 1997), Third Printing, 2004

32.   Josephy, Alvin M. Jr., *The Civil War in the American West*, Vintage Books, A Division of Random House, Inc., New York, NY, 1991

33.   Kaelin, Celinda Reynolds and the Pikes Peak Historical Society, *American Indians of the Pikes Peak Region,* Arcadia Publishing, Chicago, Illinois, 2008

34.   Kaelin, Celinda Reynolds, *Pikes Peak Backcountry, The Historic Saga of the Peak's West Slope,* Caxton Press, Caldwell, Idaho, 1999

35.   Kessler, Ronald E., *Anza's 1779 Comanche Campaign*, 2nd Edition, Adobe Village Press, Monte Vista, CO, 2001

36.   Leckie, William H. with Leckie, Shirley A., *The Buffalo Soldiers, A Narrative of the Black Cavalry of the West,* University of Oklahoma Press, Norman, OK, 2003

37.   Lanza, Ruth Willett, *Scott Kelly, Man of Mystery, True West Magazine,* courtesy of the Colorado Springs Pioneers Museum, February 19, 1989

38.   Litvak, Dianna, *El Pueblo History Museum, A Capsule History and Guide*, Colorado Historical Society, Denver, CO, 2006

39.   Mann, Charles C., *1491 New Revelations of the Americas Before Columbus*, Vintage eBooks, Random House, Inc., New York, 2011

40.   Marsh, Charles S., *People of the Shining Mountains, The Utes of Colorado*, Pruett Publishing Company, Boulder, CO

41.   Mathews, Carl F. and Matthews, E.C., *Pioneers Early Days Around the Divide,* Sign Book Company, St. Louis, MO, 1969

42.   Martinez, Wilfred O., *Anza and Cuerno Verde Decisive Battle,* Second Edition, Mother's House Publishing, Colorado Springs, CO, 2004

43.   McConnell Simmons, Virginia, *Bayou Salado,* Published by the University Press of Colorado, Boulder, CO, 2002

44.   McConnell Simmons, Virginia, *The Ute Indians of Utah, Colorado, and New Mexico,* Published by the University Press of Colorado, Boulder, CO, 2000

45.   McKenna, James A., *Black Range Tales,* Rio Grande Press, Inc., Chicago, IL, 1965

46.   Merry, Robert W., *A Country of Vast Designs,* James K. Polk, the Mexican War, and the Conquest of the American Continent, Simon & Schuster, New York, NY, 2009

47.   Millard, Candice, *Destiny of the Republic, A Tale of Madness, Medicine and the Murder of a President,* Doubleday, Random House, New York, NY, 2011

48.   Monaghan, Jay, Editor-In-Chief, *The Book on the American West,* Bonanza Books, Crown Publishers Inc., New York, NY, 1943

49.   Monahan, Sherry, *Pikes Peak Adventures, Communities, and Lifestyles, Images of America,* Arcadia Publishing, Charleston, SC, 2002

50.   Murphy, Jan Elizabeth, *Outlaw Tales of Colorado,* Morris Book Publishing, Guilford, Connecticut, 2012

51.   Olson, Robert C., *Speck The Life and Times of Spencer Penrose,* Western Reflections Publishing Company, Lake City, CO, 2008

52.   Peters, De Witt C., M.D., Late Assistant Surgeon General, U.S.A., *The Life and Adventures of Kit Carson, the Nestor of the Rocky Mountains, from Facts Narrated by Himself,* W.R.C. Clark & Company, New York, NY, 1953

53.   Pettit, Jan, *Utes The Mountain People,* Johnson Books, Boulder, CO, 2012

54.   Perkins, James E., *Tom Tobin, Frontiersman,* Adobe Village Press, Monte Vista, CO, 2005

55.   Pierson, Francis J., *Summit of Destiny, Taming the Pikes Peak Country 1858-1918,* Charlotte Square Press, Denver, CO, 2008

56.   Pryor, Alton, *The Real Story of "Kit" Carson*, Stagecoach Publishing (Smashwoods Edition), Roseville, CA, 2011

57.   Rockwell, Wilson, *The Utes a Forgotten People*, Western Reflections Publishing Company, Montrose, CO, 2006

58.   Ruhtenberg, Polly King & Smith, Dorothy E. Henry McAllister, *Colorado Pioneer*, Pine Hill Press, Freeman, South Dakota, 1971

59.   Santoro, Nicholas J., *Atlas of the Indian Tribes of North America and The Clash of Cultures*, University, Inc., Bloomington, New York, 2009

60.   Shaara, Jeff, *Civil War Battlefields, Discovering America's Hallowed Ground*, Ballantine Books, New York, 2006

61.   Sides, Hampton, *Blood and Thunder, An Epic of the American West,* Anchor Books (eBooks), Random House, LLC., Knopf Doubleday Publishing Group, 2006

62.   Smith, Anne M., *Ute Tales, Volume 29* of the University of Utah, Publications in the American West, University of Utah Press, Salt Lake City, UT, 1992

63.   Smith, David P., *Ouray, Chief of the Utes, The Fascinating Story of Colorado's Most Famous and Controversial Indian Chief,* Wayfinder Press, Ridgeway, CO, 1990

64.   Sprague, Marshall, *Newport in the Rockies,* Swallow Press, Ohio University Press, Athens, Ohio, Fourth Edition, 1987

65.   St. Clair Robson, Lucia, *Ride the Wind, The Story of Cynthia Ann Parker and the Last Days of the Comanche*, Ballantine Books, Random House, New York, NY, 1982

66.   Stokka, Terry, *A Brief History of Bridle Bit Ranch in Black Forest, Colorado, El Paso County*, Colorado, January 2005

67.   Sun Bear, Wabun Wind and Chrysalis Mulligan, *Dancing with the Wheel, The Medicine Wheel Workbook,* A Sun Bear Book, A Fireside Book, Published by Simon & Schuster, New York, NY, 1991

68.   The Pikes Peak Guy, *365 Days of Pikes Peak*, Pikes Peak Guy Press, Woodland Park, CO, 2011

69.   Thomas, Alfred Barnaby, *Forgotten Frontiers, A Study of the Spanish Indian Policy of Don Juan Bautista de Anza, Governor of New Mexico 1777-1787*, From the Original Documents in the Archives of Spain, Mexico, and New Mexico, University of Oklahoma Press, Second Printing, Norman, OK, 1969

70.   Ubbelohde, Carl & Benson, Maxine & Smith, Duane A., *A Colorado History* (8th Edition), Pruett Publishing Company, Boulder, Colorado, 2001

71.   Utley, Robert M., *The Story of the West, A History of the American West and Its People,* DK Publishing Inc., New York, New York, 2013

72.   Virga, Vincent and Grace, Stephen, *Colorado, Mapping the Centennial State Through History, Rare and Unusual Maps from the Library of Congress*, the Morris Book Publishing, LLC., Guilford, CT, 2010

73.   Von Ahlefeldt, Judy, *Thunder, Sun and Snow, A History of Colorado's Black Forest*, Century One Press, Colorado Springs, Colorado, 1979

74.   Wells, Don & Diane, *Mystery of the Trees*, 2nd Edition, Mountain Stewards Publishing Company, Jasper, GA, 2012

75.   West, Elliott, *Contested Plains, Indians, Goldseekers, and the Rush to Colorado*, University Press of Kansas, Lawrence, Kansas, 1998

76.   Whiteley, Lee, *The Cherokee Trail, Bent's Old Fort to Fort Bridger*, The 1999 Merrill Mattes Brand Book, Volume XXXIII, Published by the Denver Posse of Westerners, Inc., Johnson Printing, Boulder, CO, 1999

77.   Williams, Jack R., *American Indian Culture Trees, Living History,* Colorado Outdoor Education Center, Florissant, CO, Copyright 2001 – Revised 2012

78.   Wismer, David A. with Wright, Gary T., *Shamrock Ranch, Celebrating Life in Colorado's Pikes Peak Country*, Johnson Books, Boulder, Colorado, 2009

79.   Wroth, William, *Ute Indian Arts & Culture, From Prehistory to the New Millennium*, Published by the Taylor Museum of the Colorado Springs Fine Arts Center, 2000

80.   Ziegler, Gary R. & Malville, J. McKim, *Machu Picchu's Sacred Sisters, Choquequirao & Llactapata*, Johnson Books, Boulder, CO, 2013

About the Author

John Wesley Anderson, El Paso County Sheriff 1995-2003 (retired) has lived in the Pikes Peak Region since 1956 and grew up in the shadow of Pikes Peak on a ranch in eastern El Paso County where he loved riding horses and collecting arrowheads. John enjoyed a thirty-year law enforcement career, with the Colorado Springs Police Department and two four-year terms as the elected Sheriff for El Paso County. Much of John's law enforcement experience involved being a homicide detective, and teaching criminal investigations and forensic science. He is a graduate of the FBI Law Enforcement Executive Development Seminar and earned an MBA from Regis University. After being term-limited as Sheriff, John retired from law enforcement and went to work for Lockheed Martin, one of the world's largest defense contractors. John became recognized as an expert in the areas of Homeland Defense, Homeland Security and Corporate Security. John was given many assignments across the country and around world to include several trips to the Horn of Africa (Djibouti) and the United Arab Emeritus (Abu Dhabi and Dubai). John retired from Lockheed Martin on Columbus Day (October 12th) 2012, to launch a consulting business, JW Anderson & Associates, Ltd., and pursue his passions for history, teaching, and writing. John currently resides in Northern El Paso County, Colorado, with his wife Brenda, their daughter Laynie, a tabby cat named Jay Catsby and black lab named Mango Moose of Gleneagle.

There is a quote Jeff Broome captured in his well-researched book, Cheyenne War, Indian Raids on the Roads to Denver 1864-1869, which reads, "The Native Americans say that a story stalks a writer and, if it finds you worthy, comes to live in your heart. It is the writer's responsibility to give that story a voice." I can but hope that I have come close to fulfilling my responsibility in giving this story a voice to be heard, championing these sacred trees and the Ute, the Nuche, the people behind these trees.

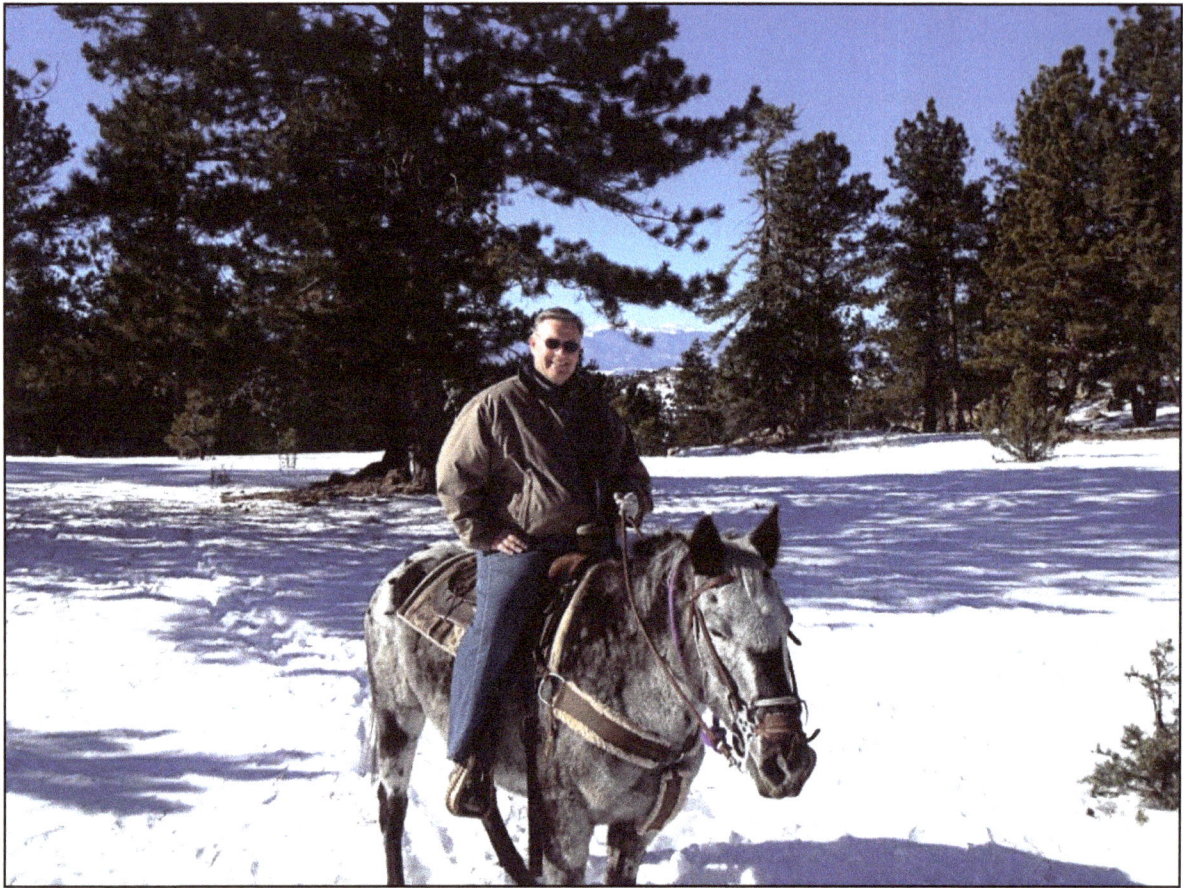

John riding the Bear Basin Ranch: This photograph is of the author riding Ole Blue across the Bear Basin Ranch with the Shining Mountains visible in the background over his left shoulder. He was in search of Ute Indian Prayer Trees with friends Joel Midkiff and ranch owners Gary Zeigler and Amy Finger. The Bear Basin Ranch is located southwest of Pikes Peak near Westcliffe, in Custer County, Colorado. Many Ute Prayer Trees were discovered during and since that exploration in 2013. Gary Zeigler, PhD., is a Colorado College graduate, noted archaeologist, geologist and author (Machu Picchu's Sacred Sisters, Choquequirao & Llactapata) who discovered numerous Culturally Modified Trees (many facing Tava) along with Native American stone artifacts on his ranch, many with astrological alignments.

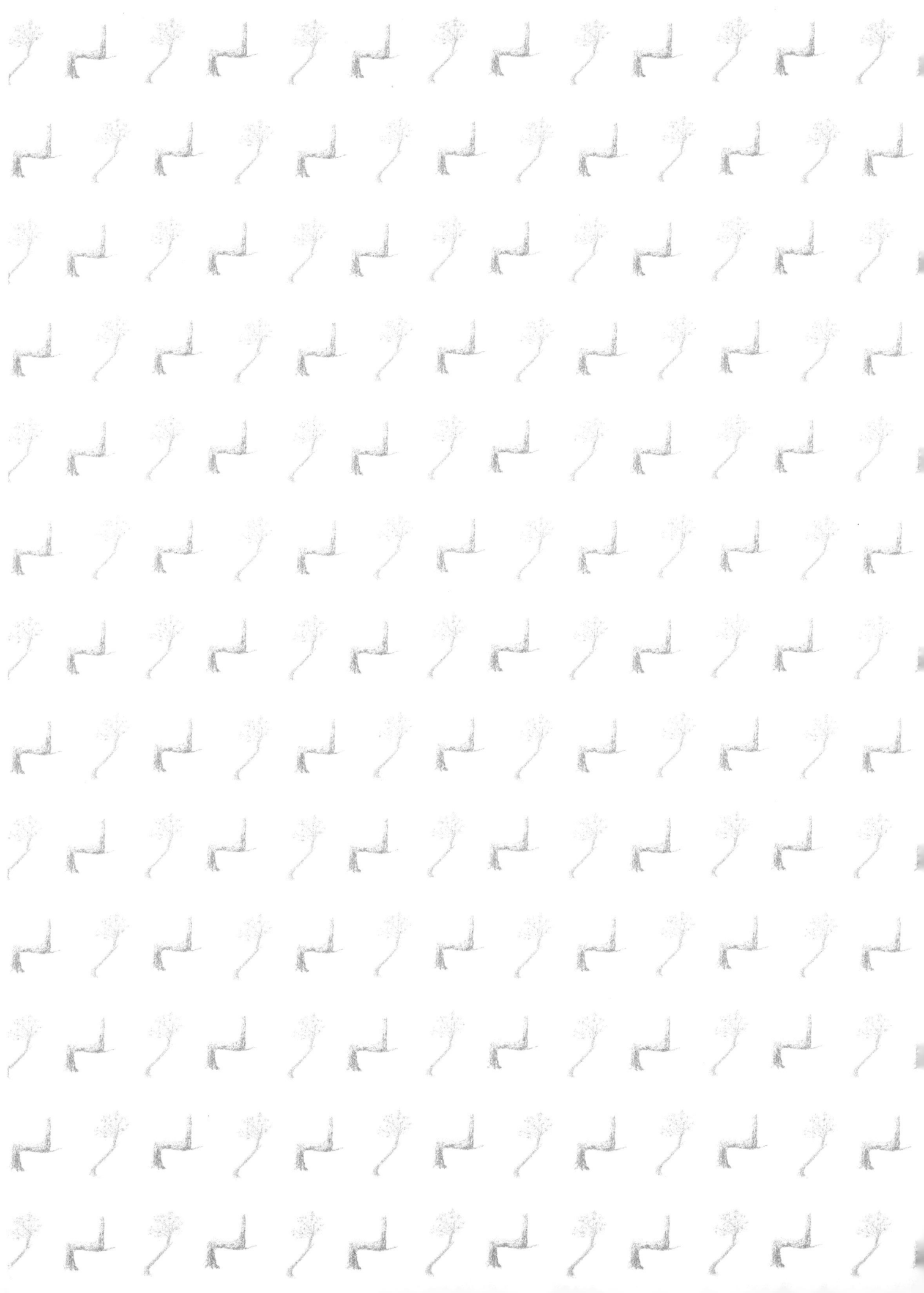

www.ingramcontent.com/pod-product-compliance
Lightning Source LLC
Chambersburg PA
CBHW061232150426

42812CB00054BA/2570